To Save the Lost

AN EASTER CELEBRATION

EDITED BY RICHARD NEITZEL HOLZAPFEL
& KENT P. JACKSON

RSC

RELIGIOUS STUDIES CENTER
BRIGHAM YOUNG UNIVERSITY

RELIGIOUS STUDIES CENTER
BRIGHAM YOUNG UNIVERSITY

Published by the Religious Studies Center, Brigham Young University, Provo, Utah
http://religion.byu.edu/rsc_rec_pub.php

Printed in the United States of America by Sheridan Books, Inc.

ISBN: 978-0-8425-2728-6
Retail U.S. $14.95

Cover painting by Sir Edward John Poynter, *The Prodigal's Return*, Brigham Young University Museum of Art

Cover design by Kristin McGuire

CONTENTS

Special thanks to Frank and Mary Ann McCord.

ABOUT THIS BOOK

*T*his volume contains the papers delivered at the 2008 and 2009 Brigham Young University Easter Conferences. The annual Easter Conference, sponsored by the Religious Studies Center, is a celebration of the life and atoning mission of Jesus Christ. Drawing not only from the Bible but also from the unique perspectives of the Restoration, papers delivered at the Easter Conference seek both to elucidate the Savior's ministry through scholarship and to bear witness of that ministry through praise and testimony. We are indebted to those who have shared their scholarship and their testimonies in this volume. We are honored to have among them Elder Merrill J. Bateman, emeritus member of the Seventy, and Bonnie D. Parkin, former general president of the Relief Society of The Church of Jesus Christ of Latter-day Saints.

We give special thanks to Frank and Mary Ann McCord of Everett, Washington, and San Diego, California. The McCords, whose generous donation made this book possible, are true friends of BYU's Religious Education and the Religious Studies Center.

Frank serves as the chairman of the Religious Education National Advancement Council. In addition to supporting us with generous contributions, he and Mary Ann dedicate hours to establishing Friends of Religious Education chapters around the country.

Mary Ann and Frank support Religious Education at BYU "because it provides a unique opportunity to spread the message of the Restored Gospel by extending the talent, knowledge, and spirit of some of the best qualified authorities in the Church who teach religion classes daily." They believe that "additional funding enables us to provide clear, accurate information regarding the history, doctrines, beliefs, and practices of the Church more effectively, creatively, and thoroughly so as to strengthen the faith and testimony of the faithful while enlightening and uplifting members and nonmembers alike."

We appreciate the McCords and others like them whose contributions bless our teaching, outreach, scholarship, and publication efforts.

It is our hope that Religious Studies Center publications will bless the Latter-day Saints through gospel-centered scholarship that incorporates the best of study and faith. Our hope for this volume is that it will help bring the spirit of Easter into the hearts of those who read it and that it will bear testimony to the mission of our Savior, Jesus Christ.

TO THE LEAST, THE LAST, AND THE LOST

Richard Neitzel Holzapfel & Kent P. Jackson

A strong theme in the scriptures is reversal. We are often surprised as the meek, instead of the powerful, inherit the earth (see Matthew 5:5), a Gentile centurion submits to the authority of Jesus, a lowly Jew (see Matthew 8:5–13), and God reveals his will to "babes" instead of the wise (Matthew 11:25). In a truly amazing scene, a dignified landholder sets aside his pride of position and runs to embrace his returning son (see Luke 15:20). However, the most important reversal of all is this: the Son of God dies so humanity can live (see Mark 14:24).

Jesus' mission—to the least, the last, and the lost—is built on such reversals. His redemptive work facilitated them, as shown in the fact that the primary meaning of *repent* in the biblical languages Hebrew and Greek is "turn around" or "return." Through the gospel, the least become the greatest in the kingdom of God (see Luke 9:48), the last become the first (see Matthew 19:30), and the lost are found (see Luke 15:32).

Easter is a good time to recall Jesus' mission to the least, the last, and the lost, for he said, "The Son of man is come to save *that which was lost*" (Matthew 18:11; emphasis added). Not surprisingly, we discover that he sent his disciples to the "lost sheep" (Matthew 10:6), and thus their mission of finding the lost is a natural extension of his. We, who desire to be his disciples in the latter days, gladly embrace our part in that mission, and we are reminded of his words that are at the very core of living the gospel: "Inasmuch as ye have done it unto one of the least of these my brethren, ye have done it unto me" (Matthew 25:40).

Some of Jesus' most memorable teaching moments have to do with finding the lost. Luke preserves the parables of the lost sheep, lost coin, and lost son and ties them together with a common theme—the joy of finding that which is lost. He introduces them by providing the historical context: Jesus was meeting with people who were considered wicked and unclean—publicans and sinners. As in other such settings, the Pharisees and scribes begin to complain, "This man receiveth sinners, and eateth with them" (Luke 15:2).

Luke tells the story: "And he spake this parable unto them, saying, What man of you, having an hundred sheep, if he lose one of them, doth not leave the ninety and nine in the wilderness, and go after that which is lost, until he find it? And when he hath found it, he layeth it on his shoulders, rejoicing. And when he cometh home, he calleth together his friends and neighbours, saying unto them, Rejoice with me; for I have found my sheep which was lost" (Luke 15:3–6). The second parable continues the theme: "What woman having ten pieces of silver, if she lose one piece, doth not light a candle, and sweep the house, and seek diligently till she find it? And when she hath found it, she calleth her friends and her neighbours together, saying, Rejoice with me; for I have found the piece which I had lost" (Luke 15:8–9).

These parables have nothing to do with sheep or coins, of course, but with the finding of lost souls. What they do not include is much detail about what it took to find what was lost, what efforts were expended, how many tears were shed and prayers uttered. Both stories reveal a common conclusion: there is joy in heaven over one "sinner that repenteth" (Luke 15:7, 10). And both teach that whatever was required to find the lost sinner was worth it.

The final parable presents the theme in human form. In English, tradition has imposed upon it the unfortunate title "Prodigal Son"—*prodigal* meaning "wasteful," the least important element of the parable. It is really the story of a lost son, and it speaks to us today as well as it did to the disciples in Jesus' day.

A Jewish father has two sons. The younger asks the father for his inheritance and departs to a far country, a Gentile land, where he "wasted his substance with riotous living" (Luke 15:13) and ends up destitute. The next scene reveals the consequence of his bad choices: "He went and joined himself to a citizen of that country; and he sent him into his fields to feed swine" (Luke 15:15). The reversal is complete: the Jewish son of a land-rich father is forced to become a hired servant of a Gentile, feeding pigs! Yet when it seems the lost son has descended as low as he possibly could, we discover that matters are indeed worse. He has to compete with the pigs for food. Finally "he came to himself," and he decides to return to his father, where even the "hired servants" have "bread enough and to spare" (Luke 15:17).

At this point in the story, we may be tempted to think, "I'm glad I'm not like him." Yet the story has enough parallels with everyone's life that we should be able to see something in it about us. At the very least, we, on occasion, need to "come to ourselves" and decide to return to what we, like the lost son, know to be right. And if we are teachable, we too will learn that our own resources are used up, that we have nothing left, and that we must rely on the grace of someone greater to welcome us back to his family and home.

The lost son returns to his father, saying, "I have sinned against heaven, and in thy sight, and am no more worthy to be called thy son" (Luke 15:21). In another reversal of the plot, the father chooses to "bring the best robe, and put it on him; and put a ring on his hand, and shoes on his feet" (Luke 15:22). Further, like the owners of the lost sheep and the lost coin, the father calls together those around him to celebrate: "Bring hither the fatted calf, and kill it; and let us eat, and be merry" (Luke 15:23).

Now the parable reveals a story within a story, and it too is a reversal. The dutiful elder son has returned from a day's labor in the field to discover music and dancing at his father's house. When a servant informs him that his younger brother has returned and received the royal treatment, the elder brother becomes angry and refuses to enter the house. For the second time, the father leaves the house to go outside to welcome a son home (see Luke 15:25–28). It seems that even the most righteous among us are in need of "pardoning mercy." And, thankfully, we are within its reach.[1]

Remember the worth of souls is great
in the sight of God;
For, behold, the Lord your Redeemer suffered
death in the flesh; wherefore he suffered the pain of
all men, that all men might repent and come unto
him.
And he hath risen again from the dead, that
he might bring all men unto him, on conditions of
repentance.
And how great is his joy in the soul that
repenteth!
(D&C 18:10–13)

As we contemplate the "lasting grace" and the "boundless charity" of our Savior,[2] let us, like those in the parables, rejoice in the finding of those who have been lost. Let us not only welcome them back, but let us help find them as well. But let us also recognize that we too are among the lost ones, always in need of one to seek us out, take us by the hand, and bring us back to our Father's home.

Notes

1. Andrew F. Ehat and Lyndon W. Cook, eds., *The Words of Joseph Smith: The Contemporary Accounts of the Nauvoo Discourses of the Prophet Joseph* (Provo, UT: Religious Studies Center, Brigham Young University, 1980), 77.

2. Lee Tom Perry, "As Now We Take the Sacrament," *Hymns* (Salt Lake City: The Church of Jesus Christ of Latter-day Saints, 1985), no. 169.

Carl Heinrich Bloch, *Christ Healing the Sick at Bethesda*,
Brigham Young University Museum of Art.

LESSONS FROM THE ATONEMENT

Elder Merrill J. Bateman

*T*he great sacrifice wrought by the Lord Jesus Christ for the sins of humankind is the most important event in time and eternity. The Atonement is the centerpiece of the Father's plan of happiness for His children. It makes possible the operation of mercy that saves and exalts the Father's children while satisfying the demands of justice (see Alma 42:15).

In planning our sojourn on earth, Heavenly Father understood the importance of agency for our progress and provided it as a gift. He also knew that Adam and Eve would transgress by using their agency to bring about the Fall in order that "men might be; and . . . that they might have joy" (2 Nephi 2:25). But the Fall would also bring death—both physical and spiritual. As mortals, the body would age and eventually die as the spirit

---

Elder Merrill J. Bateman *is an emeritus Seventy and president of the Provo Utah Temple.*

separated from it. Spiritual death, a separation from God, would occur as a result of the Fall and as men and women succumbed to opposition and temptation. Given agency, all would sin and "come short of the glory of God" (Romans 3:23).

In order to be saved from the Fall and from our sins, it was necessary that someone with sufficient power come to the rescue. Amulek, Alma's companion, stated that neither man nor any other earthly thing had sufficient power to redeem. Salvation was possible only through "an infinite and eternal sacrifice" of the Son of God (Alma 34:10; see also v. 14). Lucifer, a son of the morning, offered to be the son who would save us. But his plan was insufficient, his motives were contrary to the laws of heaven, and he lacked the power and glory to do so (see D&C 76:25–27; Moses 1:11–18; 4:1–4).

Jesus Christ, the Beloved Son, was chosen from the beginning because of His righteous nature, which led to His eventual anointing and receiving glory from His Father (see Isaiah 60:2; 1 Peter 1:19–20; Helaman 5:11; Moses 1:14). Ultimately, the Savior received all power from the Father, infinite and eternal, sufficient to pay the price of sin. In humility and suffering beyond the capacity of any human, He said to the Father, "Thy will be done, and the glory be thine forever" (Moses 4:2; see also Matthew 28:18; John 17:2).

Peter, James, and John saw the Lord in the fullness of His glory on the Mount of Transfiguration. For two and one-half years, they had traveled the byways of Israel with Him without fully appreciating His greatness, even though they believed in Him. A few months before His Crucifixion, the Savior took the three men to the top of a mountain and there revealed Himself in all His "glory as . . . the only begotten of the Father . . . full of grace and truth" (John 1:14). As the Only Begotten in the flesh, He had the power to lay down His life and take it up again. From His mortal mother, Mary, He received the seeds of mortality that allowed Him to die. From His immortal Father, He received the seeds of immortality and the capacity to overcome death and live forever. As He said to the Jews, "As the Father hath life in himself; so hath he given to the Son to have life in himself" (John 5:26).

On another occasion, Christ stated: "Therefore doth my Father love me, because I lay down my life, that I might take it again. No man taketh it from me, but I lay it down of myself. I have power to lay it down, and I have power to take it again. This commandment have I received of my Father" (John 10:17–18).

Only Christ had the power to overcome physical death both for Himself and for us. Only Christ had the power to redeem us from our sins. He inherited the power from His Father to carry out the Atonement. In mortality, He lived a sinless, perfect life. He satisfied the demands of justice for Himself, and His infinite and eternal capacities allowed Him to pay the debts for those who exercise faith in Him, repent, obey the laws of the gospel, and receive the ordinances of salvation.

A reading of the nineteenth section of the Doctrine and Covenants reveals the incongruity of a sinless God confronting the physical and spiritual pains associated with the sins of others as He "was wounded for our transgressions, . . . [and] bruised for our iniquities" (Isaiah 53:5). The Lord said: "For behold, I, God, have suffered these things for all, that they might not suffer if they would repent; but if they would not repent they must suffer even as I; which suffering caused myself, even God, the greatest of all, to tremble because of pain, and to bleed at every pore, and to suffer both body and spirit—and would that I might not drink the bitter cup, and shrink—nevertheless, glory be to the Father, and I partook and finished my preparations unto the children of men" (D&C 19:16–19).

Christ's suffering began in the Garden of Gethsemane and was completed on the cross. He prayed fervently in the garden that the Father, if willing, might remove the cup, but then acknowledged, "not my will, but thine, be done" (Luke 22:42). An angel appeared in the garden to strengthen Him. But the agony was relentless and caused Him to pray even "more earnestly" (Luke 22:44). As He moved from the garden to the trial and then to the cross, the time came when the burden was His alone. About six hours into the ordeal at Golgotha, the Savior cried with a loud voice, "My God, my God, why hast thou forsaken me?" (Matthew 27:46). A short time later, the Redeemer of the world cried again with a loud voice, "Father, into thy hands I commend my spirit: and having said thus, he gave up the ghost" (Luke 23:46). As the prophet Nephi saw in the vision of the tree of life, Christ was "lifted up upon the cross and slain for the sins of the world" (1 Nephi 11:33).

On the third day following His burial in Joseph of Arimathea's tomb, He rose from the dead. His death and Resurrection make it possible for all who have lived or will live on this earth to be resurrected and brought back into the presence of God to be judged. Thus, He overcame physical death, one of the consequences of Adam's transgression, to provide resurrection unconditionally for all people. Still, each individual is accountable for his or her own sins. Fortunately, Christ has the power to forgive and sanctify because He mercifully paid the price for those who exercise faith in Him, repent of their sins, keep their covenants, and receive the ordinances of the gospel.

The story of the Atonement is one of miracles. We do not fully understand the resurrection process or how He stands as a proxy for us in assuming our sins. We do know, however, that there were many eyewitnesses of His Resurrection and that other spirits were reunited with their bodies following Christ's Resurrection. The scriptures state that "the graves were opened; and many bodies of the saints which slept arose" (Matthew 27:52). We also know through the witness of the Holy Spirit that He is the Redeemer of the world and has the power to wash us clean, to satisfy broken laws, and to sanctify and prepare us to be lifted up by the Father (see 3 Nephi 27:14).

There are major lessons to be learned from the marvelous events associated with the Atonement. The lessons concern the importance of prayer, the role of faith and testimony in fulfilling one's eternal purpose, the importance of love as a motivating force, the role of sacrifice and obedience in obtaining spiritual power, and the opportunity afforded by the Atonement to build a strong, righteous community.

THE IMPORTANCE OF PRAYER

The first lesson from the Lord's sacrifice in Gethsemane and on the cross concerns prayer. Throughout His ministry, the Lord taught His disciples to pray. He taught them to "pray for them which despitefully use you," to "pray to thy Father . . . in secret," and to "use not vain repetitions" (Matthew 5:44; 6:6, 7). He provided the Lord's Prayer as an example (see Matthew 6:9–13). He prayed both in private and in public (see Matthew 14:23;

19:13). Prayer was an indispensable part of His life. He intended the same for His disciples. The admonition was to "ask," "seek," and "knock" (Matthew 7:7).

Undoubtedly, the most intense prayers offered by the Savior occurred following the Last Supper. The first was the great Intercessory Prayer given before He and the disciples departed for Gethsemane. In the prayer, Christ noted that His hour had come and asked for strength that He would glorify the Father in giving eternal life to the faithful (see John 17:1–2). The remainder of His prayer was devoted to His followers. He prayed for their faithfulness that they might be inheritors of eternal life. He asked the Father to bless them with the glory and love that He had received. Uppermost in the Lord's thoughts was the unity the disciples would display. Their unity would be a sign to others that the Father had sent the Son (see John 17:3–18).

The second prayer began in Gethsemane. Leaving eight of the disciples at the entrance and asking them to pray, Jesus took Peter, James, and John a little further into the garden. Instructing them also to pray, He went a stone's throw further and fell on His face, being "sorrowful and very heavy" (Matthew 26:37). He prayed, saying, "Father, if thou be willing, remove this cup from me: nevertheless not my will, but thine, be done" (Luke 22:42). His understanding and recognition of the redemptive process led to even more earnest prayer with "great drops of blood falling down to the ground" (Luke 22:44).

The final prayer occurred on the cross with the conclusion, "Father, into thy hands I commend my spirit: and having said thus, he gave up the ghost" (Luke 23:46).

Why did the Creator of heaven and earth, the Only Begotten of the Father, the Savior and Redeemer of the world, need to pray? Did He not know all things? Was He not omnipotent? John the Beloved testified that Jesus did not receive a fullness when born into mortality but "received grace for grace" and grew from "grace to grace, until he received a fulness" (D&C 93:12–13). In submitting His will, He knew the importance of communicating with the Father. Even He needed comfort! Even He needed to pray for strength!

How important is prayer for us? Clearly, if prayer was a critical part of the Savior's life, it is important in our lives. Prayer in the name of the Son is the door through which we access the Father. It is the means by which we express gratitude and receive guidance and direction. We receive the power to change our lives through prayer and obedience. Through prayer we ask the Father to help us forgive others and to bless them. Through prayer we express our earnest desires to endure to the end and return to the Father through the mercy and grace of His Son. The Lord set the example for us throughout His life and during His final hours. The Redeemer became our Advocate with the Father as a result of the Atonement. Prayer brings the Holy Spirit into our lives, and His guidance keeps us on the path into the celestial kingdom. Prayer is essential for one to stay on the strait and narrow path and the Lord was the great Exemplar.

FAITH IS THE POWER

The second lesson learned from the Atonement concerns the importance of faith. All will be saved from one of the effects of the Fall, physical death, because of the Lord's Resurrection. Both the just and the unjust will come forth from the grave (see John 5:28–29).

In contrast, overcoming spiritual death is conditional and occurs as a result of our faith in the Father and the Son, faith in Their plan, and faith in the restored gospel. Faith is referred to not as a blind allegiance but as a strong belief that leads to repentance and obedience to gospel principles. Belief and obedience are then rewarded with quiet assurances from the Holy Spirit that the Father and Son live, that They have a plan, and, as part of that plan, the gospel has been restored through the Prophet Joseph Smith. The assurance comes in the form of feelings in the soul and enlightenment to the mind as one fasts and prays, reads the scriptures, serves in the kingdom, and is diligent in living the gospel (see Alma 17:2–3; 32:27–43).

The development of faith and testimony has a pattern. The Lord told the Prophet Joseph Smith that "to some it is given by the Holy Ghost to know that Jesus Christ is the Son of God, and that he was crucified for the sins of the world. To others it is given to believe on their words, that they also might have eternal life if they continue faithful" (D&C 46:13–14).

The common pattern is that the strong assist the weak. At the beginning of a new dispensation, angels are sent to teach prophets and provide them with spiritual truths so that they, in turn, may prepare others (see Moroni 7:30–31). For example, the experiences Joseph Smith had with Moroni; John the Baptist; Peter, James, and John; and others prepared him to teach and share gospel truths so those who listened might believe on his words. As members believed and acted on the principles taught, the Spirit confirmed their belief. In like manner, parents are expected to teach their children the fundamental principles of the gospel. At first, children believe on the words of their parents, but eventually they receive their own witness if they are obedient to the principles and ordinances.

One of the great stories in the Book of Mormon that illustrates how faith develops is the appearance of the resurrected Lord to the Nephites following His Crucifixion and Resurrection in Jerusalem. In reviewing the story from 3 Nephi, it is interesting to note that the Lord began His visit with an experience, not a sermon.[1] The special experience not only prepared the Nephites for subsequent sermons but provided a spiritual foundation that would be passed down through the generations for two hundred years. The pattern was for those who received strong testimonies to help others believe on their words until the latter would receive their own assurances. A brief review of the story is useful.

Twenty-five hundred of the faithful were gathered at the temple in the land Bountiful. They were discussing the destruction and changes that had occurred earlier as well as the sign associated with the Redeemer's death. While conversing with one another, they heard a voice out of the heavens. Although they did not understand the words, they felt the Spirit pierce them to the very center (see 3 Nephi 11:3). The voice came a second time, and again they did not understand. The third time the scriptures record they "did open their ears to hear it; and their eyes were towards the sound thereof" (3 Nephi 11:5). The verses that follow indicate that they understood the words but did not fully appreciate the meaning. The words were, "Behold my Beloved Son, in whom I am well pleased, in whom I have glorified my name—hear ye him" (3 Nephi 11:7). As they looked into the heavens, they saw a "Man descending . . . clothed in a white robe; and he came down and stood in the midst of them;

and the eyes of the whole multitude were turned upon him, and they durst not open their mouths, . . . for they thought it was an angel" (3 Nephi 11:8). Not fully appreciating who the visitor was, they stood in awe.

Christ then introduced Himself and told them He had partaken of the bitter cup and "glorified the Father in taking upon [him] the sins of the world" (3 Nephi 11:11). As the multitude listened, they realized the visitor was the resurrected Lord, and they fell to the earth. The experience that followed changed their lives forever as the Lord beckoned them to arise and come forward one by one to feel the prints of the nails in His hands and feet and to thrust their hands into His side. The scripture reads, "And this they did do, going forth one by one until they had all gone forth, and did see with their eyes and did feel with their hands, and did know of a surety and did bear record, that it was he, of whom it was written by the prophets, that should come" (3 Nephi 11:15).

The opportunity to see, hear, and touch the Lord, supported by a witness from the Holy Ghost, gave impressions, thoughts, and feelings that were never forgotten. In turn, the faith and testimony of those present sunk deep into the hearts of their children, grandchildren, and great-grandchildren as future generations were impacted by their parents' testimonies. By believing on the words of their parents, the children could gain a testimony just as strong as their parents' if they combined their belief with obedience to the commandments. Living the commandments opens the heart for the Holy Spirit to confirm the belief. One should remember the Lord's words to Thomas: "Because thou hast seen me, thou hast believed: blessed are they that have not seen, and yet have believed" (John 20:29). Why?

Because faith based on the words of others combined with a spiritual assurance from the Holy Spirit may be as powerful or even more powerful than faith based on eyesight.

Faith in Christ is key to receiving access to a fullness of the Lord's Atonement. Those who inherit the celestial kingdom are those "who [receive] the testimony of Jesus, and [believe] on his name," enter into His covenants, and keep His commandments (D&C 76:51–52). In contrast, those assigned to the terrestrial kingdom, the honorable men and women of the earth, receive "not the testimony of Jesus in the flesh" and are "blinded by the craftiness of men" (D&C 76:74–75). These good people are offered a witness of the truth but do not have the faith to receive it. Just as the Savior exercised His faith in the Father and submitted His will to God in order to complete His mission, so we will accomplish our earthly purposes through our faith in Them.

LOVE AS THE MOTIVATION

The third lesson from the Atonement is the importance of love as a motivating force. It is easier to understand one sacrificing one's own life to save others than to sacrifice the life of one's son. And yet "God so loved the world, that he gave his only begotten Son, that whosoever believeth in him should not perish, but have everlasting life" (John 3:16). God's love for His children was the motivating force that forged the Atonement. Part of the plan was to do everything possible to extend mercy and save His children without destroying the gift of agency.

Christ's love for His brothers and sisters was as deep as the Father's. As the Good Shepherd, He was willing to give His life for the sheep. The hireling would flee when the wolf comes, but not the Good Shepherd, who knows the sheep (see John 10:11–15). The Savior said to His disciples, "Greater love hath no man than this, that a man lay down his life for his friends" (John 15:13). The pure love of Christ for His brothers and sisters led Him into the garden and on to Golgotha even though He could call down legions of angels to protect Himself (see Matthew 26:53).

Jesus expects no less of His disciples. A restatement of the law on love was given by the Savior following the Last Supper. The old commandment received by Moses and repeated earlier to a group of nonbelievers by Jesus was to "love thy neighbour as thyself" (Matthew 22:39). Following the Last Supper, Jesus raised the standard when He said, "A new commandment I give unto you, That ye love one another; as I have loved you, that ye also love one another. By this shall all men know that ye are my disciples, if ye have love one to another" (John 13:34–35).

As disciples, we are to love others as Christ loves us, not as we love ourselves. Deity's love for us defines the way we must love. We are to become like Them (see Matthew 5:48; 3 Nephi 27:27). The expectation is that we will love not only those who love us but also our enemies, those who despitefully use us and those who persecute the Saints (see Matthew 5:44–47). Moreover, a sign of our love is that we keep the commandments. Jesus said, "As the Father hath loved me, so have I loved you. . . . If ye keep my commandments, ye shall abide in my love; even as I have kept my Father's commandments, and abide in his love" (John 15:9–10).

Near the end of His ministry, Christ told the Twelve that in the last days "because iniquity shall abound, the love of many shall wax cold" (Matthew 24:12). Paul describes the same condition in his second letter to Timothy: "This know also, that in the last days perilous times shall come. For men shall be lovers of their own selves, . . . without natural affection" (2 Timothy 3:1–3). In contrast, the Lord is building a Zion people who are striving to have a Christlike love for one another and for all men. And the Atonement, by changing people's hearts, makes it possible. Christ exemplified love throughout His life, but the greatest acts of love occurred in the Garden of Gethsemane and on the cross.

OBEDIENCE IS THE PRICE

The fourth lesson to be learned from the Lord's Atonement is the importance of obedience to the gospel plan. A few years ago, I became familiar with a mission motto that outlined gospel principles in relation to the Atonement. The motto is as follows:

> Faith is the power,
> Obedience is the price,
> Love is the motive,
> The Spirit is the key,
> And Christ is the reason.[2]

Thus far we have discussed faith as the power to access the conditional blessings of the Atonement and love as the motivator that should guide our actions as evidenced by the Father's willingness to sacrifice His Son. In order to develop faith and receive the power that flows from it, the price is obedience.

From the beginning Adam was taught the associated principles of sacrifice and obedience. Upon leaving the Garden of

Eden, Adam and Eve were given a commandment to offer the "firstlings of their flocks, for an offering unto the Lord. And Adam was obedient unto the commandments of the Lord" (Moses 5:5). After some time, an angel appeared unto Adam and asked why he was offering sacrifices. Adam responded that he did not know except the Lord had commanded him. The angel then taught him about the Atonement and that the sacrifice was in the "similitude of the sacrifice of the Only Begotten of the Father" (Moses 5:7).

When Moses brought the children of Israel out of Egypt to the mount, the Lord called the prophet to the top of the mountain and gave him counsel for Israel. The Lord said: "If ye will obey my voice indeed, and keep my covenant, then ye shall be a peculiar treasure unto me above all people: for all the earth is mine: and ye shall be unto me a kingdom of priests, and an holy nation" (Exodus 19:5–6).

Israel was promised three blessings conditioned upon their obedience. They would become a special people, they would receive the fullness of the priesthood, and they would become a holy nation (see 1 Peter 2:9). Unfortunately, they were not prepared to pay the price, and a lesser law was substituted. It would be more than a thousand years before the fulness of the gospel and the higher priesthood would be given to the people of Israel.

If there is one lesson to be learned from the Savior's life, it is the Son's submissiveness to the Father, His desire to be obedient. On one occasion He said, "I do nothing of myself; but as my Father hath taught me" (John 8:28). In the great Intercessory Prayer, Christ said, "I have finished the work which thou gavest me to do" (John 17:4). In Gethsemane, He said, "Not my will, but thine, be done" (Luke 22:42). The Savior was wholly devoted to accomplishing the mission given Him by the Father in the premortal world.

We reap what we sow. If we want to be saved and exalted, the price is obedience. If we are halfhearted in living the commandments, the reward will not be a full measure. We will be judged according to our "works, according to the desire of [our] hearts" (D&C 137:9).

Elder Neal A. Maxwell has written: "The submission of one's will is really the only uniquely personal thing we have to place on God's altar. The many other things we 'give,' . . . are actually the things He has already given or loaned to us. However, when you and I finally submit ourselves, by letting our individual wills be swallowed up in God's will, then we are really giving something to Him! It is the only possession which is truly ours to give!"[3]

A ZION PEOPLE

The fifth and final lesson concerns the establishment of a Zion people—a righteous people with all things in common (see Moses 7:18). From the beginning, the Lord has worked to establish a community of Saints where righteousness would be a leavening agent for the world. It began with Adam and Eve. They were taught the gospel of Jesus Christ and were told to teach it to their children "that all men, everywhere, must repent" (Moses 6:57). In time, apostasy prevailed, and the Lord began again with Noah and his family. Abraham's call and the formation of the house of Israel created the foundation for building a righteous kingdom, but Jacob's descendants also fell into apostasy.

From the midst of the burning bush, Moses learned that he was to return to Egypt and reclaim Israel in another effort to sow the seeds of righteousness.

The Lord's parable of the wicked husbandmen in Mark 12 describes the many attempts by the Lord to establish Zion. Again and again, the Lord of the vineyard sends His servants to collect the fruit. Some servants were wounded, while others were killed. Finally, the owner of the vineyard sends His Son, His Well-Beloved, saying, "They will reverence my son" (Mark 12:6). But the husbandmen say, "This is the heir; come, let us kill him, and the inheritance shall be ours" (Mark 12:7). The husbandmen take the Son, kill Him, and once again thwart the effort to build Zion. The Lord concludes the parable by indicating that the owner of the vineyard will destroy the husbandmen and give the vineyard to others.

Just as periods of apostasy occurred following the stoning and death of earlier prophets, a great apostasy followed the death of the Son and of the Apostles. Eventually, other servants were called to reestablish the vineyard—the story of the restored gospel.

The establishment of the Church and the kingdom of God on the earth in the last days is the final effort. This time the kingdom will never be destroyed. The prophet Daniel saw the kingdoms that followed Nebuchadnezzar's down to the last days. Near the end he sees the "God of heaven set up a kingdom, which shall never be destroyed: and the kingdom shall not be left to other people, but it shall break in pieces and consume all these kingdoms, and it shall stand for ever" (Daniel 2:44).

Nephi also saw the kingdom of God in the last days. The Saints were scattered upon all the face of the earth, and even though their numbers were small, Nephi sees the "power of the Lamb of God" descend "upon the saints of the church of the Lamb, and upon the covenant people of the Lord, . . . and they were armed with righteousness and the power of God in great glory" (1 Nephi 14:14).

Since the early 1800s, the Church has operated under the mandate to take the gospel to every nation, kindred, tongue, and people. For the first century, new converts were encouraged to gather to a Zion in order to build a center place of strength. By the 1960s that foundation was in place, and members were encouraged to remain in their own lands to build Zion there.

The Church population today is about thirteen million, which is still small in relation to the earth's six-plus billion. Even if the Church grows to one hundred or two hundred million during the decades ahead, Church membership will still be relatively small. Nevertheless, the righteous influence of the Church, flowing from members who have faith in the Lord's Atonement and are obedient to God's commandments, is making and will make a mark in the world. It is beginning to happen in various communities as Saints live faithful, righteous lives and assume leadership roles. The effects of well-organized groups of Saints were seen when Hurricane Katrina hit the southern United States. It has been seen in Florida, Oklahoma, California, Brazil, Peru, and Indonesia.

In financial terms the Church a modest player on the world's humanitarian stage; however, it is becoming one of the largest private contributors. In terms of manpower, however, the Church is a major force. There are few private organizations that can muster thousands or even tens of thousands of well-organized members in times of crisis. The Church is one organization that can assemble large numbers because of the faith of its members. Whether the devastation is caused by a hurricane, an earthquake, a tsunami, or some other catastrophe, the Church is able to organize a tremendous force to assist in the recovery effort. The world is beginning to recognize us as a people armed with God's power in righteousness. Again, the Atonement is at the center as we assist the Lord in building a Zion people. It is why we are concerned about the welfare of others.

CONCLUSION

The Lord's Atonement is unique. Its reach is infinite and eternal. The Atonement required the life of the Son of God. The first key lesson to be learned from the Savior's life is the importance of prayer. Even though Christ was the Jehovah of the Old Testament, the Creator of heaven and earth, the Only Begotten in the flesh, His communication with the Father was critical in completing His mission. In a similar manner, prayer to the Father through the Son provides the guidance we need in order to complete our earthly missions.

Second, faith in the Father and the Son is required for us to access the full blessings of the Lord's sacrifice. Faith opens the door for us to be cleansed and sanctified. Faith comes by exercising a belief in the Father and the Son that brings a witness from the Holy Spirit. The Savior's faith in His Father is His example for us, shown by His willingness to submit and carry out the plan.

A third lesson gleaned from the Atonement is the importance of love. Our Father is a very personal God who loves His children and will communicate with them if they strive to be open to receiving communication from Him. His love for His children was the motivating force that caused Him to send His Son to be crucified for our sins. As we, His children, exercise faith in this kind, loving God, we too will be motivated by love in our relationships.

The fourth lesson focuses on obedience. The Son submitted His will to the Father's. Ultimately, we show our love for and loyalty to the Father through our submission and obedience to the Lord's commandments. Fortunately, the Atonement allows our deviations from the path to be corrected through faith and repentance.

Finally, brothers and sisters, we have a responsibility to help the Lord build a Zion people in order to leaven the whole earth. May we contribute to this task with lives filled with faith, prayer, love, and obedience. In turn, we will receive a full measure of the blessings granted by the Lord's sacrifice.

NOTES

1. At a recent stake conference in the Provo Utah Grandview East Stake, President Richard Williams shared this insight.

2. Cyril Figurerres, Japan Fukuoka Mission motto.

3. Neal A. Maxwell, in Conference Report, October 1995, 30.

Giuseppe Mazzola, *Holy Family (Adoration)*,
Brigham Young University Museum of Art.

FAMILY AND HOME IN THE SAVIOR'S LIFE AND MINISTRY

S. Kent Brown

A fair question arises: on Easter, why turn to a topic such as family and home in the Savior's life and ministry? My presentation, I hope, will answer this question. Family and home are so deeply embedded in the story of Jesus that, upon review, it becomes clear he is concerned with them from the beginning to the end of his ministry. And in that story we dare not bracket his Atonement.

Luke's Gospel account opens with a series of stories that feature the home, and each in some way touches upon the Savior. As a preface, I observe that the first mention of place in the Gospel is the sanctuary. Luke writes about the priest Zacharias, "He went into the temple of the Lord" (Luke 1:9). With this note, Luke confers a sense of holiness across his two books, the

---

S. Kent Brown *is a professor emeritus of ancient scripture at Brigham Young University.*

Gospel and the book of Acts. Within this holy environment, we meet the angel Gabriel, who comes to Zacharias and prophesies about a child. We hear his words: "Thy prayer is heard; and thy wife Elisabeth shall bear thee a son, and thou shalt call his name John" (Luke 1:13). Hence, in this scene, the sanctuary and the family or the home become linked together, forming an interwoven whole as the story proceeds. But this experience is only the beginning. Bound into this bundle, John's birth makes the family of Zacharias and Elisabeth complete.

We can imagine that when Zacharias and Elisabeth are married, wonderful expectations abound for them. Friends, neighbors, and family members see in them rich possibilities: children and grandchildren. But then one long year passes another, and no children come. I suspect that Elisabeth especially faces many questions such as "What is wrong with me?" Certainly her neighbors would have been asking, "I wonder what's wrong with her? What has she done to earn the Lord's disfavor?" For, as we know, barrenness is often seen in her society as a sign of God's disfavor. Then comes the moment when all changes. Elisabeth's words are, "He [the Lord] looked on me, to take away my reproach" (Luke 1:25). One senses worlds of meaning in her words. Moreover, we feel the gracious healing hand of the Lord in two words that Luke pens: "Elisabeth conceived" (Luke 1:24). In sum, we feel the hand of the Lord moving his majestic work forward—in the home.

The themes of home and family continue in a setting almost exactly sixty-five miles north of the temple. Recalling the layer of holiness that lies across Luke's text because he features Zacharias in the sanctuary, we now come to what we call the "Annunciation," the scene in which the angel Gabriel finds Mary in her home.

How do we know that he finds her there? The text reads, "The angel came in unto her" (Luke 1:28). The Greek text actually repeats a participle and says, "coming inside toward her." Thus the angel comes into a place where Mary feels secure and private. She is frightened because of that intrusion, hence the angel says to her, "Fear not, Mary" (Luke 1:30). The angel's message has to do with a child, a child who will begin her family and become a part of her home. The story of this encounter illustrates that a home can become a place of revelation and a place of God's miracles.

Mary also responds to the news from the angel about her distant cousin's pregnancy. She learns from the angel that Elisabeth is now almost six months along, "behold, thy cousin Elisabeth, she hath also conceived a son" (Luke 1:36), and she senses the imperative in the angel's words to go visit her cousin. Significantly, by Mary's coming to Elisabeth's home, we find that the two homes now become physically connected.

The scene next switches to the home of Elisabeth and Zacharias in what people have come to call the "Visitation." Both women are watched by God. Certainly God looks out for Mary as she leaves her own home and goes to the place near Jerusalem where Elisabeth lives. When these two women come together at Elisabeth's home, it is as though the Spirit cannot withhold and descends richly upon them, and we hear the first of Elisabeth's welcoming words, "Blessed art thou among women" (Luke 1:42). The babe leaps in her womb, underscoring that the infant is "filled with the Holy Ghost from his mother's womb" (D&C

84:27; see also Luke 1:15), which also testifies of Elisabeth's goodness and worthiness before the Lord.

Remarkably, through inspiration, Elisabeth becomes the first witness of the virgin birth. We hear her words: "There shall be a performance of those things which are told her [Mary] from the Lord" (Luke 1:45). She knows by inspiration that something special is happening to her young cousin. Elisabeth therefore becomes the herald of the mother of God's Son, as her son will serve as herald of Christ. All of this occurs at Elisabeth's home. In addition, other special Spirit-driven events occur inside her home: Mary gives voice to her inspired song, "The Magnificat" (Luke 1:46–55); Zacharias' mouth is miraculously opened in their home after John's birth (Luke 1:64); Zacharias sings his inspired song, "Benedictus," in their home (Luke 1:68–79). One conclusion is that their home has become a spiritual powerhouse, much like the temple.

One added note: the secret of the ages, who the mother of the Son of God will be, has now first been entrusted to two women. As far as we are aware, no one else on earth yet knows.

Here I shift gears to look at Mary as Jesus' mortal mother and to suggest that hints lie inside the text which talk about the strength and the normality of her home life with the young Savior. Many readers of the Gospels notice that Joseph is missing from the scenes of Jesus' ministry. The usual conclusion—correct in my view—is that Joseph has passed away. But his influence remains in an interesting passage. In Mark 6:3, Jesus is called by acquaintances "the carpenter." It becomes apparent from this little aside that Joseph has taught Jesus his trade. Joseph's skills as an artisan—an ability to work with wood, stone, and metal—

has been passed to Jesus.[1] In addition, he has taught Jesus how to work.

In the very same verse, Mark 6:3, Jesus is also called "the son of Mary." This name honors her, implying a strong, honorable mother. People in their community knew her as an honorable woman. And thus they placed her name on her Son when they talked about Him as "the son of Mary."[2]

A further important detail arises out of Luke 4. The Nazareth townspeople are surprised at the powers that reside in this young man who has grown up in their midst. They have recently heard of the miracles that he performed down at Capernaum (Luke 4:23). Such a detail tells us that Jesus grows up in a normal home where, as a boy in his society, he learns to pray and to read and to work. Clearly, his mother and his adoptive father raised him in a strong, clean, devoted environment.

Jesus' healings now come into view. More often than not, his healings carry an immediate impact into someone's home. We start with Luke chapter 5, wherein Jesus meets a man "full of leprosy" and heals him (see Luke 5:12–14). Because of his disease, this man is exiled from home and friends. He is never clean. He can never shake hands with anyone. He can never go into anyone's home. He is distant from all and has to keep his distance from all. When Jesus heals him, he literally brings him back to his home. It is warming to think that this man, who has been off by himself all these years and estranged from family members, now is reunited with them.

Luke chapter 6 reports a story about a man with a withered right hand whom Jesus heals in a synagogue. Again, this man is unclean, for he is left to perform all tasks for himself with his left hand, including bodily functions and eating. He is not a person whom anyone will invite to dinner in a home. Why? Because he brings uncleanness with him, and everything he touches is rendered unclean. Healing him heals his relationship with his family, and with his friends beyond them.

In Nain, a town in Galilee, Jesus approaches a funeral procession as it comes out of the town and stops it. There he finds that the only son of a widow has died (see Luke 7:11–16). This woman's only claim to help, to income and support, comes from this son. But now death has taken him from her. To be sure, she still has her dowry, but she has no legal claim on anyone else for support. In addition, this young man has died without posterity; he is not yet married. So she is completely alone. By raising her son from the dead, Jesus gives back to the widow her child and future grandchildren so that her physical needs will now be met and her name will live on among her descendants, into eternity.[3]

The Gadarene demoniac is a man who lives in tombs, wears no clothes, and screams. People have tried to tie him up, but he breaks the cords. He is a total embarrassment to his family. Jesus now comes across the lake to the east side, into Gentile territory. This man is a Gentile, not a Jew. After encountering the man, Jesus heals him (see Luke 8:26–39). In the aftermath, the man begs Jesus to allow him to follow Him. And Jesus says, no. These are his words—"Return to thine own house" (Luke 8:39). We can only imagine what it is like for his family to receive him back. Furthermore, Jesus places him in a spot where, over time, not only do people learn about this man's healing, but they come to respect the power behind his healing. Their first response, of course, after seeing what Jesus has done, is to ask Jesus to leave. They are frightened by what has happened and are frightened by the enormous power required to control this man (see Luke 8:37). But over time, this man will show that he has regained his normalcy. Then, when Jesus sends the seventy into Gentile territory and some come back to that town, the seed is already planted and a harvest of souls will occur. People will respond to the message that the seventy bring.

Of course, Jesus' healing the woman with the issue of blood will have an impact on her family (see Luke 8:43–48). Because she has been unclean for twelve years, she cannot go to the synagogue or to the temple. She renders everything in her house unclean in a ritual way. A person cannot accept a loaf of bread or a jug of milk from her, because she renders it unclean. At the moment of her cleansing, things change for her and for her family.

The same thing happens with Jairus' twelve-year-old daughter (see Luke 8:41–42, 49–56). By giving life to this young girl about to step into adulthood, the only child of Jairus and his wife, Jesus gives back to them their future and their family. I want to add a further note. We remember that, when Jesus arrives at the home, it is already filled with well-meaning neighbors and friends and family members who have already begun to mourn and, in accordance with custom, to wail. The noise is so loud in the home that Jesus does what any good leader should in preparing for a spiritual experience—He invites the noise to leave. He sends all those people outside, thereby creating a space of quiet and calm and peace wherein he can call down the power of God and raise this young girl from the dead.

I turn to another story wherein concern for family lies just out of sight. But if we think about it, the family stands in full view. The first few verses of Luke 5 tell us of Peter's unusual experience on the shore of the Sea of Galilee. The account concludes with the call of Peter and his brother, Andrew, as well as their partners, James and John, who follow Jesus as disciples (see Luke 5:1–11). The report opens with a crowd that is following Jesus. He has come down to the seashore, and there is no easy way that he can talk to everybody unless he can put some small distance between Himself and them. He sees Peter in his boat and basically asks, "May I get into your boat and talk to these people?" Jesus climbs in, sits down and, from a few feet offshore, addresses the whole crowd. At the end of this little sermon, Jesus turns to Peter and asks, "How is fishing?" Peter answers, "Really lousy. We fished all night and didn't catch a thing." We know that Peter has been sitting and listening to this whole sermon while cleaning his nets. Jesus then says, "Row over there and throw out your nets." We also know that somebody besides Peter is in the boat, for a series of plural pronouns stands in the account (see Luke 5:5–7). It could be his brother Andrew. Not only are they listening to what Jesus is saying in the boat, but a few days before they are standing in their own home and watching as Jesus raises Peter's mother-in-law from illness. So they are inclined to do as Jesus suggests. They throw out the net, and it fills with fish. Then they call to their partners, who come with their boat, and they load the fish into both boats, almost sinking them by the end of this experience.

Lest we think this haul is a small catch of fish, I turn our minds to the fact that, in 1986, when the Sea of Galilee was especially low, some people found a fishing boat from the right era just off the northwest shore in the mud of the lake. The discoverers were smart. They sensed what they had and actually found a way to enclose it, lift it out of the mud, and put it into a chemical bath to preserve it. You can still see the boat in a museum in the nearby town. The boat measures 24.5 feet in length, 7.5 feet wide, and 4.5 feet deep. This boat will hold a lot of fish before it is driven to the bottom of the lake.[4] The fish that Peter and his brother catch and load into the two boats make up a huge amount.

So where does family come into all of this? Actually, they are close by. Jesus' subsequent act of asking these men to follow Him will take the breadwinners out of the midst of their families. After all, they fish for a living. And, it seems to me, one can correctly ask the question, "What about their families as they become full-time disciples?" The answer rests in the fish. A person might say, "Yes, but in twenty-four hours the fish will begin to spoil. The families cannot eat all of them in that much time, and they cannot sell them in that much time. There just aren't enough people in the town to buy all those fish." Strabo, an ancient geographer who died less than ten years before Jesus began his ministry, notes that just down the coast from Capernaum, about four and a half miles, lies a notable town that came to be known as Magdala, the hometown of Mary Magdalene. In this town there is a fish salting industry where, if family members will row their boats, they can have all those fish preserved.[5] The families will now have many months' supply of food, plus they have enough fish that they can sell and make money to meet other needs. Hence, within the miracle of the fish, just before he calls these men to be his disciples, Jesus leaves the source of support for their families. He does not leave them bereft.

I turn attention to another set of accounts that occur later in Luke's Gospel. We start with the scene of Jesus as a guest at a dinner hosted by Martha in her home and joined by Mary, her sister. This story occurs at the end of chapter 10 (Luke 10:38–42). A number of patterns come together in this report. I draw two into sight. One of them has to do with the setting of a home, and the other has to do with prayer. A person may ask, "Where does prayer appear in this story?" It shows up in Martha's importuning Jesus to say something to Mary so that she helps with the meal. That sort of importuning stands very close to prayer: begging the Lord for help, asking Him for his assistance.

Now we step into chapter 11. Here the first thirteen verses have to do with prayer. At first, we find the Lord's Prayer. Then we find a number of other sayings of Jesus that have to do with how one should pray. Finally Jesus talks about home. Luke introduces the subject of home in an interesting way. He reports that many observe Jesus casting out a demon that has rendered the victim dumb or unable to speak (see Luke 11:14). Some are amazed at the miracle, but others in the crowd say, "I bet he is casting demons out by the chief of demons, Beelzebub." Then follows a conversation about this idea. In it, Jesus responds that a kingdom divided cannot stand, that a house divided against a house cannot stand (see Luke 11:15–20). Therefore, the house is very much a part of what Jesus is talking about.

Next Jesus utters a saying about a strong man who sits in his palace, comfortable and secure. But when a stronger one comes, the stronger dispossesses the strong one and takes over the home (see Luke 11:21–22). We ask ourselves, what does all that mean? Then Jesus follows that example with a saying about an unclean devil that "walketh through dry places," looking for a place to live after he is tossed out of his home. He comes back to the original place he was living, finds it "swept and garnished," runs off, grabs seven of his terrible friends, brings them back, invades the place, and they take up residence there. Jesus makes the point that the man's state is worse in the latter instance than it was before, clearly applying this scene to a person who is in trouble (see Luke 11:24–26).

At this point, let me back up and suggest an interesting sequence that flows out of this series of stories, starting with Mary and Martha, next with his teaching on prayer, then his broad discussion about Satan's kingdom and devils and evil influences. Commentators, including Elder James E. Talmage, have noticed the story of the strong one in the house and the stronger one who pushes him out. They see Satan in the strong one and Jesus in the stronger.[6]

Let me suggest to you that a series of teachings about the home falls out of these stories. First, home becomes and is rightly a place of prayer. Martha's beseeching Jesus for help is an illustration of that. Second, the home is a place of unity, which Martha's temporarily is not. In Jesus' words, the divided home falls, the divided home fails. Third, the home invaded by evil, by the strong one, can only be cleansed by inviting in the stronger one. In effect, the home becomes the place where the struggle between good and evil occurs.

In light of these three points, let us make a general observation. We can leave our homes as they are. But if evil is present, we run a serious risk. Through prayer, we can invite in the stronger one. The Savior, when invited, can come and displace the strong one, the devil, and keep him at bay. We see that, somehow, lying amidst the banter of Jesus with his opponents and rising within his sayings to them, the home stands in close proximity to the world of evil, so close that this world both forms an inimical and crippling intrusion into the home and must be overcome and separated from it. In effect, without a conquering effort, evil can make its permanent camp within a person's home. The story of the wandering spirit illustrates the point most graphically: it pines for its lost home and, when opportunity arises with help, pushes its way back inside, thus disrupting the home's sacred and tranquil character. In my view, these stories are to be seen as a whole, fitting tightly together and illustrating Jesus' concern for a harmony in the home that rests on proper spiritual principles, as Jesus' words about Mary demonstrate: "One thing is needful: and Mary hath chosen that good part" (Luke 10:42).

In sum, our review has taken us across a large aggregate of stories and sayings, events and small details that lie embedded in Luke's Gospel. Taken together, they underscore the enormous importance of family in the Savior's life and ministry. Much of what he says and does purposely carries an impact into someone's home. What happens inside family and home matters, in time and in eternity, as he tries to teach and demonstrate in his ministry. His Redemption, whose seeds are sown in events leading to his birth, grows complete in his life and ministry as he shows concern and compassion for homes and families.

NOTES

1. The term translated "carpenter" (Greek *tektōn*) is the general term for a skilled artisan (Walter Bauer, *A Greek-English Lexicon of the New Testament*, trans. William F. Arndt and F. Wilbur Gingrich, rev. F. Wilbur Gingrich and Frederick W. Danker, 2nd ed. [Chicago: University of Chicago Press, 1979], s.v. "tektōn").

2. S. Kent Brown, *Mary and Elisabeth: Noble Daughters of God* (American Fork, UT: Covenant Communications, 2002), 73–74.

3. Eryl W. Davies, "Inheritance Rights and the Hebrew Levirate Marriage," *Vetus Testamentum* 21 (1981): 138–44, 257–68; James R. Baker, *Women's Rights in Old Testament Times* (Salt Lake City: Signature Books, 1992), 51, 134, 137, 140; Ze'ev Falk, *Hebrew Law in Biblical Times* (Provo, UT, and Winona Lake, IN: BYU Press and Eisenbrauns, 2001), 109–10, 153–55.

4. Shelley Wachsmann, *The Sea of Galilee Boat: An Extraordinary 2000-Year-Old Discovery* (New York: Plenum Press, 1995).

5. Strabo (64 BC–AD 21) writes, "At the place called Taricheae [Magdala] the lake supplies excellent fish for pickling" (*Geography* 16.2.45). Taricheae lay about four and one-half miles southwest of Capernaum and three miles north of Tiberias; also Emil Schürer, *The History of the Jewish People in the Age of Jesus Christ*, 3 vols., rev. ed. by Geza Vermes, Fergus Millar, and Matthew Black (Edinburgh: T. & T. Clark, 1973–1987), 2:69–70, on Taricheae as a center for pickling. Significantly, the name *Taricheae* is related to the Greek term *tarichos*, which means "dried or salted fish" (Henry George Liddel and Robert Scott, eds., *A Greek-English Lexicon*, rev. ed. Henry Stuart Jones [Oxford: Oxford University Press, 1940], 1758).

6. James E. Talmage, *Jesus the Christ* (Salt Lake City: Deseret Book, 1945), 268; Leon Morris, *Luke: An Introduction and Commentary*, rev. ed. (Grand Rapids, MI: Eerdmans, 1988), 217.

Max Thalmann, *Last Supper*,
Brigham Young University Museum of Art.

WAR AND PEACE— LESSONS FROM THE UPPER ROOM

Kent P. Jackson

*T*hree days before his Crucifixion, Jesus sat with the Twelve on the Mount of Olives and spoke with them of the future. He warned them that the world would be an increasingly hostile place for them, and the same would be true for other Saints of their time and for his disciples in the latter days as well. As he taught them, he spoke of apostasy, betrayal, hatred, false prophets, false Christs, abounding iniquity, and declining love (see Joseph Smith—Matthew 1:6, 8–10). His message regarding the Apostles themselves was anything but a happy one. "Then shall they deliver you up to be afflicted," he said, "and shall kill you, and ye shall be hated of all nations, for my name's sake" (Joseph Smith—Matthew 1:7).

Kent P. Jackson *is a professor of ancient scripture at Brigham Young University.*

The Cenacle, or Upper Room, Jerusalem. Photos courtesy of Kent P. Jackson.

In Jerusalem today, there is a medieval Roman Catholic chapel in a building constructed by the Crusaders to mark the sites of events from the Bible. The room represents for millions of pilgrims the upper room in which Jesus met with his disciples the evening before his Crucifixion. We call that meeting the Last Supper. In the most intimate conversation with the Twelve recorded in the New Testament, Jesus spoke with them about things to come and about how they were to carry on through the difficult times that lay ahead for them. He warned them again, in very clear language, that the world would hate them. Such would be the case because the Apostles, like all Christians, were not of the world. People would kill them, he said, thinking that in doing so they would be doing God a favor (see John 15:18–19; 16:2). Yet with pointed irony, in words that are as surprising in this context as they are reassuring, Jesus concluded his discussion by saying, "These things I have spoken unto you, that in me ye might have *peace*. In the world ye shall have tribulation: but be of good cheer; I have overcome the world" (John 16:33; emphasis added).

LIVING IN DAYS OF WARS AND RUMORS OF WARS

The scriptures call our time "days of wickedness and vengeance" (Moses 7:60). We experience in these days much tribulation, and thus, like Jesus' ancient disciples, we need to learn how to have peace in spite of it. We witness "wars, and rumors of wars" (Joseph Smith—Matthew 1:23), and we experience many other evils and sorrows that God's children have brought upon themselves. The Book of Mormon teaches us how to live in such troubled times. It is not an accident that Mormon provided only twenty-three verses for the two-hundred-year period of peace following Jesus' visit to the children of Lehi (see 4 Nephi 1:1–23), yet he wrote twenty chapters about warfare covering only fifteen years (see Alma 43–62). Those chapters are followed by more that recount a droning litany of political intrigue, conspiracies, murder, war, apostasy, betrayal, economic collapse, and societal decline and dissolution (see Helaman 1 through 3 Nephi 7). Mormon clearly wanted his latter-day readers to learn how to endure faithfully in a world of turbulence and tragedy, because he knew that many of us would live in such a world.

War is not the only tribulation that humanity faces today. But we focus on it because it has been such a common part of world history in modern times and because it continues to plague us now. We need to learn how to live in days like these.

37

War is from Satan, and peace is from God. In the Book of Mormon, we learn that righteous people never start wars. War sometimes comes upon people who do not deserve it but are subjected to it because of the wickedness of other people. Perhaps paradoxically, the book praises both those who are forced to defend themselves militarily and also those who made a covenant never to bear arms and who would rather die than shed the blood of their brothers. In the Book of Mormon, we learn that those who initiate wars often proclaim high-minded principles, such as the righting of past wrongs (for example, see Alma 54:17–18; 3 Nephi 3:10). Yet the book exposes their true motives to be those most common, but devil-like, human traits: hatred and the desire for power (see Alma 2:10; 43:7–8; 46:4; 51:8; Helaman 2:5). The Book of Mormon teaches that men may defend themselves when attacked (see Alma 43:46–47), but it condemns preemptive military action, even against wicked people who desire to do us harm (see 3 Nephi 3:20–21). The only time righteous people in the Book of Mormon enter "enemy" lands is when they do so to teach their brothers and sisters the gospel (see Alma 26:23–26). The Book of Mormon shows that missionary work among intractable foes is a more successful means of neutralizing their threats than is waging war against them (see Alma 31:5; Helaman 5:20–52; 6:37).

Given human nature, war may be inevitable, but how one responds to it is a conscious choice between discipleship on the one hand, and following the ways of the world on the other. History has shown that politicians can easily invent justifications for military aggression, and they can stir up crowds to cheer the start of a war and to enlist to fight in it. But Latter-day Saints, like Jesus' ancient disciples, are not of the world, and thus we can never really be part of it and its ways. Our scriptures are clear: we are commanded by God to "renounce war and proclaim peace" (D&C 98:16), and righteous nations are only allowed to engage in military action—always with sorrow and profound reluctance—to protect their homes, their liberties, their families, and their religion, and to protect weaker peoples under their care. This is the law of war that the Book of Mormon teaches so clearly (see Alma 27:21–24; 43:9–10, 45–47). In contrast, the natural man—"an enemy to God" (Mosiah 3:19)—seeks to change other people by imposing on them by force his own vision of what is right, sometimes even rationalizing that it is for his opponents' own good.

When Jesus met with the Twelve on the Mount of Olives, he prophesied that warfare would be a common feature in the latter days, twice stating that we would "hear of wars, and rumors of wars" yet pointing out that the existence of such would not mean that the end is necessarily near (Joseph Smith—Matthew 1:23, 28). The implication seems to be that wars and the tragedies that accompany them would be a predictable characteristic of the world in which we live—not exceptional events. This surprises no one, because humanity has witnessed warfare and murder in the past hundred years on a scale greater than anyone could have imagined before. My ninety-three-year-old father has lived through the most devastating man-made disasters in human history—World Wars I and II—and also the Korean and Vietnam Wars, two wars in Iraq, and various other conflicts. In addition to these wars that involved the United States, his lifetime has coincided with unspeakable atrocities that rulers have imposed upon their own people and countless other wars, conflicts, and genocides that have taken a toll in human suffering and sorrow beyond comprehension. Despite the lessons we should be learning from history, virtually all those who started these tragedies, whether they won or lost, were hailed by their own as heroes, and monuments were built in their honor. Truly, as Jesus foretold of our time, "iniquity shall abound," and "the love of men shall wax cold" (Joseph Smith—Matthew 1:30).

Not all of the tribulations that people experience in the latter days will be caused by war and political unrest. But because these will likely remain with us now and in future generations, we need to learn how to deal with them. Like the ancient disciples who were tutored by Jesus during the last days of his mortality, we want to know, how can we live in a world of wars and rumors of wars and not be of it? How can we have peace?

The gospel teaches that we *can* have peace. If Jesus were with us today, how would he address us in light of the challenges we face? Perhaps he would say to us what he said to them. To learn from his words, let us enter the upper room and join the ancient disciples to be taught at Jesus' feet.

WHY WILL WE HAVE PEACE?

Jesus said, "Peace I leave with you, my peace I give unto you: not as the world giveth, give I unto you. Let not your heart be troubled, neither let it be afraid" (John 14:27). This passage has great power because its words so dramatically transcend the somber setting in which they were spoken, with warnings of rejection, persecution, wars, and murder. Yet despite all this, Jesus promised them peace. It would not be the peace of the world; it would be *his* peace. And it would be such that if they would embrace it, they would not need to have troubled hearts, nor would they need to fear.

On that evening in the upper room, Jesus gave his Apostles the solution by teaching them four reasons why they—and we—can have peace. Each of the reasons prepares us and fortifies us. Each provides a key whereby we can have peace in spite of the world. First, we can have peace because Jesus went ahead to prepare a place for us; second, because he has revealed the Father to us; third, because he does not leave us comfortless; and fourth, because he taught us how to love.

"I go to prepare a place for you" (John 14:2). Jesus said, "In my Father's house are many mansions: if it were not so, I would have told you. I go to prepare a place for you" (John 14:2). Belief in an afterlife better than this life places hope in the hearts of millions of people and enables them to endure and persevere through life's trials. Most religions teach, in one form or another, that our stay here is temporary and preparatory and that it will be worth it in the next life to live properly in this one. The Prophet Joseph Smith taught, "What have we to console us in relation to our dead? We have the greatest hope in relation to our dead of any people on earth. We have seen them walk worthy on earth, and those who have died in the faith . . . have gone to await the resurrection of the dead, to go to the celestial glory."[1] But Jesus' statement teaches much more than a happy life after death. The mention of "many mansions"—more accurately translated "rooms" or "dwelling places"—suggests the doctrine of varying degrees of glory, something confirmed in revelations to Joseph Smith (see D&C 76). The Prophet once gave a paraphrase that broadens our perspective: "In my Father's kingdom are many kingdoms."[2]

Jesus said, "When I go I will prepare a place for you, and come again, and receive you unto myself, that where I am ye may be also" (Joseph Smith Translation, John 14:3).[3] When we read that Jesus was about to leave the earth to prepare for our arrival in heaven, we sometimes focus on the verb *prepare* that he used. He was going ahead to prepare a place for us. Perhaps we might imagine him going to our new mansion, opening the big doors,

Jesus and the Bitter Cup, Church of St. Mary Magdalene, Jerusalem.

arranging the furnishings, and making it ready for our coming. But is that where Jesus went so we could have a place with him in the Father's kingdom? Notice his words to the Prophet Joseph Smith, which describe where he went and the full nature of the preparations he undertook there in our behalf: "For behold, I, God, have suffered these things for all, that they might not suffer if they would repent; but if they would not repent they must suffer even as I; which suffering caused myself, even God, the greatest of all, to tremble because of pain, and to bleed at every pore, and to suffer both body and spirit—and would that I might not drink the bitter cup and shrink—nevertheless, glory be to the Father, and I partook and finished my *preparations* unto the children of men" (D&C 19:16–19; emphasis added).

To provide for us the most direct route to our heavenly reward, he took a dreadful detour in our behalf. His journey included the Garden of Gethsemane, where he shed blood from every pore and wished not to partake of the bitter cup. He went there so we would not have to go there.

On the slope of the Mount of Olives today is the Russian Orthodox Church of St. Mary Magdalene, built at the place that Russian pilgrims venerate as the Garden of Gethsemane. In the church, amidst the smoke of the candles and incense burners, is a painting of Jesus on his knees, praying to the Father. Above and in front of him, suspended in the air or held by unseen hands, is the bitter cup of which Jesus was to drink. The cup is not painted in true perspective but is two-dimensional, like a shadow. Jesus' eyes are riveted on the cup, and the viewer is left to interpret for him- or herself what he was thinking or saying at the moment depicted. Was it "Father, if thou be willing, remove this cup from me"? Or was it "Not my will, but thine, be done" (Luke 22:42)?

Jesus' journey to prepare our place also included Golgotha, where he suffered the unspeakable torture of crucifixion and died. Where did Jesus go in order to prepare a place for us in the Father's kingdom? We, if we die faithful, will be "taken home to that God who gave [us] life" and "received into a state of happiness" (Alma 40:12) to await a glorious resurrection. But such was not the case with Jesus.

On his journey through Gethsemane and Golgotha, Jesus descended below all things, traveling to where he did not need to go for his own sake but where he chose to go for ours. Remarkably, he did it because he loves us and wants us to be with him, "that where I am," he said, "ye may be also" (John 14:3). Or, as Joseph Smith paraphrased, "that the exaltation that I receive you may receive also."[4] As imperfect as we are without his attending grace, we should be moved to eternal gratitude to know that our perfect Savior is not satisfied unless his disciples are where he is.

Surely, a heavy price was paid to prepare a place for us. And surely, he is "the way, the truth, and the life," and "no man cometh unto the Father" but by him (John 14:6).

A fresco in the tiny Orthodox Dark Church in Cappadocia, Turkey, shows Jesus overcoming death. He stands on a vanquished Satan, who lies chained and powerless. Under Jesus' feet are the shattered remains of the gate of hell and the fetters that once bound those who were captives to sin and death. The resurrected Jesus, conqueror in his war against sin and death, lifts Adam to life out of the grave. Behind Adam, and on the other side of Jesus, are other worthy people, each one awaiting his or her turn to be taken by the hand and drawn up to salvation. We who are the beneficiaries of Christ's atoning work can have the hope that he will likewise lift us up. And this hope will bring us peace in this life—Jesus' peace—despite the tribulations of the world and the chains that bind us now.

The Resurrection, Dark Church, Göreme, Turkey.

"If you know me, you will know my Father also" (New Revised Standard Version, John 14:7). Another reason we can find peace in this world of war is because Jesus has revealed the Father to us. His teachings about God are made most important by the fact that Jews in his day had lost all knowledge of God the Father separate from Jehovah. When he proclaimed that he was Jehovah, the God of ancient Israel, he also made known the Father and revealed the true nature of the Godhead and his role in it (see John 8:58). Jesus said, "If ye had known me, ye should have known my Father also: and from henceforth ye know him, and have seen him. Philip saith unto him, Lord, shew us the Father, and it sufficeth us. Jesus saith unto him, Have I been so long time with you, and yet hast thou not known me, Philip? he that hath seen me hath seen the Father; and how sayest thou then, Shew us the Father?" (John 14:7–9).

Indeed, Christ's character is perfect and so in harmony with that of the Father that everything he said and did in mortality represented what the Father would have said or done had he been there. We do not need to see the Father, because we see the Father manifested in Christ. "Believest thou not that I am in the Father, and the Father in me?" he asked. "The words that I speak unto you I speak not of myself: but the Father that dwelleth in me, he doeth the works. Believe me that I am in the Father, and the Father in me" (John 14:10–11).

A beautiful medieval depiction of Jesus is found in a mosaic in the Byzantine Church of Holy Wisdom (or Hagia Sophia) in Istanbul. Jesus is shown in his divine role as Pantocrator—the Almighty, or Ruler of All. He has the holy scriptures in one hand and is making a gesture of blessing with the other. This is an image not of Jesus' mortality and suffering but of his Godhood.

Mosaic of Jesus as Pantocrator, Hagia Sophia, Istanbul.

The Pantocrator image is often found in high domes in Orthodox churches, so worshipers can see Jesus in his majesty high
above them. He is the perfect representation of God, "the bright-
ness of [the Father's] glory, and the express image of his person"
(Hebrews 1:3). "In him the whole fullness of deity dwells bodily"
(NRSV, Colossians 2:9).

Beyond the truths we learn about God in the upper room,
there are even greater truths made known through the Restoration of the gospel, among which is the comforting knowledge
that God truly is our Father and that we truly are his children.
Joseph Smith taught: "What kind of a being is God? . . . The
scriptures inform us that 'this is eternal life, to know the only

wise God and Jesus Christ whom he has sent' [John 17:3]. If any inquire what kind of a being God is, I would say, If you don't know God, you have not eternal life. Go back and find out what kind of a being God is." Then the Prophet said: "I will tell you, and hear it, O earth! God, who sits in yonder heavens, is a man like yourselves. That God, if you were to see him today, that holds the worlds, you would see him like a man in form, like yourselves. Adam was made in his image."[5]

We do not worship an unknown God, because Jesus has revealed him to us. We know him, we know his nature, we know his work, and we draw peace in a world of tribulation from knowing the profound truth sung around the world by Latter-day Saint children: "I am a child of God, and he has sent me here."[6] Because we know that he is a loving Father in Heaven, we trust his judgment, we trust his plan, and we know that despite the sorrows of the world, he is there for us.

"I will not leave you comfortless" (John 14:18). A third reason why we can have peace in a world at war is that Jesus has not left us alone. The Gospels suggest that the Twelve did not grasp, even on that evening before the Crucifixion, what would be happening to Jesus later that night and the next day, or how those events would dramatically change everything about their world. They would soon find themselves seemingly abandoned, leaderless, confused, and without direction. They would experience the effects of Nephi's prophecy that "the multitudes of the earth" would be "gathered together to fight against the apostles of the Lamb" (1 Nephi 11:34). But Jesus knew that the Twelve would carry forth his mission. He would not leave them alone to face the world; he would send them the Holy Spirit to be their Comforter and their Teacher. He told the Apostles, "I will pray the

Father, and he shall give you another Comforter, that he may abide with you for ever; even the Spirit of truth; whom the world cannot receive, because it seeth him not, neither knoweth him: but ye know him; for he dwelleth with you, and shall be in you" (John 14:16–17).

Little did the Twelve know at that time how vital the Spirit's presence would become in their lives, how its influence would transform them, enlarge them, and enlighten them. Among other things, it would bring back to their memory things that Jesus had taught them that they could not understand without its influence. "These things have I spoken unto you, being yet present with you," he said. "But the Comforter, which is the Holy Ghost, whom the Father will send in my name, he shall teach you all things, and bring all things to your remembrance, whatsoever I have said unto you" (John 14:25–26). Jesus told them that the Holy Spirit would be able to teach them things that they could not learn from him. "I have yet many things to say unto you," he said, "but ye cannot bear them now. Howbeit when he, the Spirit of truth, is come, he will guide you into all truth: . . . and he will shew you things to come" (John 16:12–13).

After their reception of the Holy Ghost, the Twelve were changed men. Whereas they are sometimes depicted in the Gospels as uncertain and confused, they are shown in Acts and in their letters to be powerful men with a clear vision of where the Church was going and how they would lead it there. As promised, the Holy Ghost brought things to their memory (see John 12:16) and guided them to truth (see Acts 10:1–35).

It is not incidental that Jesus called the Holy Spirit the Comforter. Many thousands of Latter-day Saints today can attest to the peace brought into their lives by the Comforter's presence. They can tell of heavy burdens they are able to lift with the Spirit's help and of knowledge and wisdom they have received under the Spirit's instruction. Latter-day Saints who have lived during earlier wars—particularly those who have fought in them—can attest to the Spirit's presence among his Saints, even in the worst of times.[7]

Joseph Smith taught: "After a person hath faith in Christ, repents of his sins, and is baptized for the remission of his sins, and received the Holy Ghost (by the laying on of hands), which is the first Comforter, then let him continue to humble himself before God, hungering and thirsting after righteousness and living by every word of God. And the Lord will soon say unto him, 'Son, thou shalt be exalted.'"[8] In the world to come, faithful Latter-day Saints will enter the divine presence, where "the keeper of the gate is the Holy One of Israel; and he employeth no servant there" (2 Nephi 9:41). There they will be found worthy and will be welcomed home by their Savior, finding ultimate peace in the assurance of eternal life. Some have had assurances while yet in this life (see 2 Timothy 4:6–8; D&C 132:49), but all who will be heirs of the celestial kingdom can feel even now the peace that Jesus brings—not the peace of the world, but knowledge from the Comforter that their course has been correct and that they were not left comfortless along the way.

"Continue ye in my love" (John 15:9). A fourth reason why we can find peace in this life is because Jesus has taught us how to love—to love both God and our fellowmen. The love of Christ brings peace. "A new commandment I give unto you," he said in the upper room. "That ye love one another; as I have loved you, that ye also love one another. By this shall all men know

that ye are my disciples, if ye have love one to another" (John 13:34–35). It should be profoundly important to us that the test Jesus gives to demonstrate true discipleship is the love we show to each other. It is likewise important that the model he gives is his own love for us: "This is my commandment, That ye love one another, as I have loved you" (John 15:12). If that is our model, we should consider seriously the extent to which Jesus was willing to show his love for us.

One of the earliest images of Jesus is of him as the Good Shepherd. A fourth-century relief from Carthage, North Africa, shows him with a lamb on his back, depicted as in the parable of the lost sheep (see Luke 15:4–6). He told his disciples, "I am the good shepherd, and know my sheep, and am known of mine" (John 10:14). His use of the shepherd imagery was not only to show that he was our leader but more to show the quality of his leadership and his love. "The good shepherd giveth his life for the sheep," he said, "and I lay down my life for the sheep" (John 10:11, 15). In the upper room, he taught, "Greater love hath no man than this, that a man lay down his life for his friends" (John 15:13).

Love is a powerful source of peace in life. Often those who love and know they are loved are the happiest of people, whereas those who do not or cannot love are the most miserable. Joseph Smith taught that love is "one of the chief characteristics of Deity" and that it "ought to be manifested by those who aspire to be the sons of God."[9] But can we love in a time of war, and are we really expected to love our enemies? Is it not easier to dehumanize them in our minds and in our speech so we do not have to think of them as God's children? Is it not more expedient politically to refuse to sit with them than it is to try to make peace with them, or even to try to bless their lives? The Book of Mormon, again, teaches conduct that is directly contrary to how nations behave today. We can learn much from the example of the sons of King Mosiah. When they, through their repentance, found Jesus' peace in their own lives, they could not rest until they had shared that peace with others. When some of their countrymen expressed dismay that they wanted to teach their "enemies" and argued instead that they should kill them, the

Jesus as Good Shepherd, Carthage, North Africa.

sons of Mosiah, in contrast, worked at great personal risk to share with them the gospel (see Alma 26:23–26). It is interesting to note that throughout the Book of Mormon, the righteous call their opposing nation "our brethren," even in times of war against them (see Jacob 7:26; Mosiah 22:3; Alma 56:46). Joseph Smith taught that one who is "filled with the love of God, is not content with blessing his family alone, but ranges through the whole world, anxious to bless the whole human race."[10] Those filled with God's love do not know national or ethnic boarders for their love. They truly believe, as Nephi taught, that "the Lord esteemeth all flesh in one," and that "all are alike unto God" (1 Nephi 17:35; 2 Nephi 26:33).

Jesus taught that another manifestation of our love for him is our desire to keep his commandments. He said, in a passage not well translated in the King James Version, "If ye love me, *ye will* keep my commandments" (John 14:15; emphasized words added). The future tense shows that obeying Jesus is a natural product of loving him, not just a response to a command. "He that hath my commandments, and keepeth them, he it is that loveth me," Jesus said (John 14:21). And "If a man love me, he will keep my words" (John 14:23).

Loving Jesus is its own reward. It brings into our lives the companionship of the Holy Ghost and the knowledge that our lives are in harmony with Jesus' will. And it brings us peace. The Savior said, "As the Father hath loved me, so have I loved you: continue ye in my love. If ye keep my commandments, ye shall abide in my love; even as I have kept my Father's commandments, and abide in his love. These things have I spoken unto you, that my joy might remain in you, and that your joy might be full" (John 15:9–11).

Peace and Joy

As we leave the upper room and consider again our own world of wars and rumors of wars, we are reminded of the causes of many of life's conflicts and of the path that leads to the peace that Jesus promised. The Book of Mormon, in an earlier time of tribulation, tells us that the warfare the people experienced "would not have happened had it not been for their wickedness and their abomination" (Helaman 4:11). Mormon provides a list of what those abominations were: pride, oppressing the poor, withholding food from the hungry and clothing from the naked, mocking that which is sacred, denying revelation, murdering, plundering, lying, stealing, committing sexual sin, and creating contention and political dissension (see Helaman 4:11–12). Needless to say, all of these are common today, and thus there is no reason why our society should boast in its own strength that we will be immune from the consequences of such things (see Helaman 4:13).

The antidote to all of this is to live the gospel. But the sad and frank reality is that the world as a whole will never again be a place of peace until the Prince of Peace comes again to receive his kingdom. In an extraordinary contribution of his New Translation of the Bible, the Prophet Joseph Smith revealed the account of Enoch's vision from his own time to the end of the world. Enoch saw Satan with "a great chain in his hand," veiling the whole face of the earth with darkness—symbols that are so stark they need no explanation. In response to the misery of the human family, Satan "laughed, and his angels rejoiced" (Moses 7:26). God, however, looked upon the scene and wept (see v. 28). How striking is the contrast in the vision between

God the Father, St. Peter in Gallicantu, Jerusalem.

God and Satan. Why did God weep? He told Enoch that he had commanded the people to "love one another"—the same "new" commandment that Jesus gave his disciples in the upper room—yet they were "without affection, and they hate[d] their own blood" (Moses 7:33).

A Catholic church in Jerusalem, St. Peter in Gallicantu, contains a striking modern mosaic showing God the Father in the heavens. He is observing, with obvious emotion, things that are happening on earth below. In his vision, Enoch saw the earth crying out, "When shall I rest, and be cleansed from the filthiness which is gone forth out of me?" (Moses 7:48). Enoch picked up the refrain himself and asked God twice, "When shall the earth rest?" (Moses 7:58; see also v. 54). The setting for the St. Peter in Gallicantu mosaic is the trial of Jesus, with the cross looming above the trial scene and the Father looking down from above the cross. God has his hand at his forehead and is filled with remorse at what he sees; perhaps he is weeping.

Enoch was told that the earth will indeed rest someday, but its rest will come only after a time of "great tribulations." Yet even in the midst of those tribulations, "my people will I preserve," the Lord said (Moses 7:61). We and our descendants are the Lord's people living in that day of great tribulations. The Lord will preserve us (see D&C 115:6).

Can we have peace and happiness in this world of violence? We can. It is interesting to note that in two Book of Mormon passages, the word *joy* is found in the context of the word *peace*. Mormon reports, "There was *peace* and exceedingly great *joy* in the remainder of the forty and ninth year; yea, and also there was continual *peace* and great *joy* in the fiftieth year of the reign of the judges." "And in the sixty and fifth year they did also have great *joy* and *peace*" (Helaman 3:32; 6:14; emphasis added). In these instances, the joy the Saints were experiencing was in brief periods of peace between wars. Another example comes from an earlier generation: "But behold there never was a happier time among the people of Nephi, since the days of Nephi, than in the days of Moroni, yea, even at this time, in the twenty and first year of the reign of the judges" (Alma 50:23). Despite the constant threat of warfare in Captain Moroni's time, the people were happy then, because they were one and they were living the gospel.

Jerusalem's Church of the Holy Sepulchre is the traditional (and most likely) place where Jesus Christ was buried and resurrected. Inside the church, there is an Orthodox chapel that may still contain remnants of the rock-cut tomb in which Jesus' body lay. On a beautiful altar cloth is embroidered a simple two-word inscription. It reads *christos anestē*, "Christ is risen."

Christ is risen, and we will be preserved and have peace in this turbulent world because he has, as he told his disciples in the upper room, overcome the world. And because he has overcome the world, we can "be of good cheer" (John 16:33). The Church of Jesus Christ will continue to roll forward despite the world, and faithful Saints, living the gospel and keeping themselves clean from the sins of their generations, will have Jesus'

Traditional tomb of Jesus, Church of the Holy Sepulchre, Jerusalem.

peace—the true peace—in their hearts and in their homes and in their lives. The warfare of the world will continue and will take its casualties, but for those who endure faithfully, the words of President Gordon B. Hinckley will be true: "We are winning, and the future never looked brighter."[11]

NOTES

1. Andrew F. Ehat and Lyndon W. Cook, eds., *The Words of Joseph Smith: The Contemporary Accounts of the Nauvoo Discourses of the Prophet Joseph* (Provo, UT: Religious Studies Center, Brigham Young University, 1980), 347; spelling, capitalization, and punctuation standardized.

2. Ehat and Cook, *Words of Joseph Smith*, 371; capitalization and punctuation standardized.

3. Thomas A. Wayment, ed., *The Complete Joseph Smith Translation of the New Testament* (Salt Lake City: Deseret Book, 2005), 246.

4. Ehat and Cook, *Words of Joseph Smith*, 371.

5. Ehat and Cook, *Words of Joseph Smith*, 343–44; spelling, capitalization, and punctuation standardized.

6. Naomi W. Randall, "I Am a Child of God," *Hymns* (Salt Lake City: The Church of Jesus Christ of Latter-day Saints, 1985), no. 301.

7. See Robert C. Freeman and Dennis A. Wright, *Saints at War: Experiences of Latter-day Saints in World War II* (American Fork, UT: Covenant, 2001), 137, 319, 351.

8. Ehat and Cook, *Words of Joseph Smith*, 5; capitalization and punctuation standardized.

9. Joseph Smith, *History of the Church of Jesus Christ of Latter-day Saints*, ed. B. H. Roberts, 2nd ed. rev. (Salt Lake City: Deseret Book, 1957), 4:226.

10. Smith, *History of the Church*, 4:226.

11.   Gordon B. Hinckley, "An Unending Conflict, a Victory Assured," *Ensign*, June 2007, 9.

Minerva K. Teichert, *Jesus at the Home of Mary & Martha*,
Brigham Young University Museum of Art.

THEY MINISTERED UNTO HIM OF THEIR SUBSTANCE: WOMEN AND THE SAVIOR

Camille Fronk Olson

arious images symbolize and typify Jesus Christ in scripture. He is Alpha and Omega (see Revelation 1:8; D&C 19:1; 35:1) and the author and finisher of our faith (see Hebrews 12:2). He personifies the love of God in the tree of life (see 1 Nephi 11:7; 15:36) and the Bread of Life in the manna in the wilderness (see John 6:31–35). Often, the typology of Christ conveys male imagery; for example, the Savior is the male lamb without blemish that is sacrificed for sin (see Exodus 12:5), the mighty man of war who conquers every enemy (see Isaiah 42:13), and the Good Shepherd, who gives his life for his sheep (see Isaiah 40:11; John 10:11; Hebrews 13:20).

Camille Fronk Olson *is an associate professor of ancient scripture at Brigham Young University.*

Other scriptural metaphors of Christ express female imagery. He is as the pained woman in childbirth, crying in anguish as she brings forth life (see Isaiah 42:14); the mother who caresses and comforts her troubled child (see Isaiah 66:13); and the mother hen who gathers her chicks under her wings (see 3 Nephi 10:4–6; D&C 10:65; Luke 13:34). The Savior's merciful mission of salvation is further linked to the pains and unselfishness of motherhood by the same Hebrew root (rhm) that produces the word for Christ's compassion and a mother's womb.

In spite of such ways that the Messiah was likened to women, Jewish society at the time of Christ did not acknowledge the value of women or consider ways that women could contribute to their religious worship. On the contrary, men in first-century Palestine frequently marginalized women and distrusted their witness. For example, on that first Easter morning, the disciples questioned the women's report of the empty tomb, concluding that their words were merely "idle tales" (Luke 24:11). Even today these New Testament women and their testimonies are easily overlooked, which obscures their potential to apply to us. This chapter will consider the Savior's sacrifice and victory over death from the perspective of these women with the hope that they may lead us to a renewed appreciation for his enabling power and promises.

A couple of general observations will be helpful in establishing the larger context for this paper.

First, a comparison of the testimonies of Matthew, Mark, Luke, and John reflects some conflicting details surrounding the witnesses of Christ's Resurrection. Attempts to perfectly harmonize the various accounts have proved disappointing except to conclude that an unspecified number of men and women in

Palestine had a personal encounter with the resurrected Lord. Who saw him first and where and when must remain somewhat nebulous.

The Nephites' witness of the resurrected Christ provides a parallel scenario in that the specific order in which they approached their Savior seems irrelevant. From the Book of Mormon we simply know that 2,500 men, women, and children came forward "one by one" to see with their eyes and feel with their hands the prints of the nails in their Redeemer's resurrected body. Each of them could thereafter bear record that he was unquestionably Jesus Christ, whom the prophets had testified would be slain for the sins of the world (see 3 Nephi 11:15–16).

My second general observation: the purpose of scripture is to testify of the Savior's victory over sin and the grave. Holy writ proclaims that none is like Jesus Christ; he alone is Redeemer and Savior. Therefore, the focus of the Gospel narratives is not to communicate that any of the disciples was more deserving, more loved, or more righteous than the other followers of Jesus. They were not written to indicate that God views an Apostle's witness with greater merit than one professed by other disciples or that a man's testimony is more valuable than a woman's. Furthermore, the scriptures do not teach that women are innately more spiritual or receptive to revelation than men, or that either men or women have less need of Christ's enabling power than the other. Rather, the scriptures jointly testify that each of us is lost and in desperate need of a Redeemer. In this way, every man, woman, and child who encountered the resurrected Lord in the meridian of time is a type of each of us. Through their individual and combined experiences, we are led to discover and proclaim our own personal witness of Jesus Christ.

THE WOMEN'S IDENTITY

Who were the women near the cross and at the empty tomb? Collectively, Matthew, Mark, Luke, and John name several women in the Passion narratives, noting that they all came from Galilee.

1. Mary, the mother of Jesus (see John 19:25)

2. Mary Magdalene, the only woman named in all four Gospels (see Matthew 27:56; 28:1; Mark 15:40; 16:1, 9; Luke 24:10; John 19:25; 20:1, 11–18)

3. Mary, the mother of James and Joses (see Matthew 27:56; 28:1; Mark 15:40; 16:1; Luke 24:10)

4. The mother of Zebedee's children (perhaps the same as number 5) (see Matthew 27:56)

5. Salome (perhaps the same person as "the mother of Zebedee's children" because they appear in nearly identical lists of women in two of the Gospels) (see Mark 15:40; 16:1)

6. Joanna, the wife of Chuza, Herod's steward (see Luke 24:10)

7. The sister of Jesus' mother (see John 19:25)

8. Mary, the wife of Cleophas (see John 19:25)

9. "And many other women which came up with him [from Galilee] unto Jerusalem" (Mark 15:41; see also Luke 23:49, 55–56)

Of all the Gospel writers, only Luke introduces us to these "Galilean women" *before* the death and Resurrection of Christ. Because Luke records few of their names in his earlier narrative, we cannot definitively conclude that the women were those at the cross. We can, however, glean general insights into those women who attended the Savior at his death and burial from a study of these women who became disciples in Galilee.

In Luke 8:1–3, we learn that in addition to Mary Magdalene and Joanna, a woman named Susanna and "many others [women]" in Galilee, received the Savior's healing from "evil spirits and infirmities." With their lives transformed, these women formed an important core to the Savior's unofficial entourage as he and the Twelve traveled "throughout every city and village" (v. 1). They were not, however, merely tagging along. Jesus and his itinerant company depended on the goodness of others to provide daily nourishment and a place to sleep. Apparently these good women assisted in the Lord's sustenance because they "ministered unto him of their substance" (v. 3), meaning they gave to him from their own resources.

The implication here is that these women had access to ample means and the freedom to divest of it in the way they deemed pertinent. They also appear to have had the support and blessing of husbands or families to be relieved of traditional domestic duties in order to serve the Savior in this way. At least one of the women, Joanna, was married. Others may have been widowed or single. One wonders at the social ramifications for a group of women who traveled around the country with Jesus and his Apostles. Did they attend the entourage during the day and return to their own homes at night? Were any of them related to one of the male disciples? Did their children ever accompany them, or had they already reared their children? Whatever the circumstance, their commitment to the Savior was not episodic; these women still followed him in Jerusalem—to his Crucifixion, his burial, and his Resurrection.

In Luke 7–8, in verses surrounding Luke's brief description of these generous women from Galilee, he recounts the stories of specific women whose lives were forever changed through encounters with the Savior. Notably, we read of the widow of Nain (see Luke 7:11–15), the woman who loved the Savior so much that she washed his feet with her tears (see Luke 7:36–50), the mother of Jesus (see Luke 8:19–21), the daughter of Jairus (see Luke 8:41–42, 49–56); and the woman who was healed of a serious illness by touching the hem of the Savior's clothing (see Luke 8:43–48).

Were these women among the Galilean ensemble that shared their resources along with Mary Magdalene, Joanna, and Susanna? Although no conclusive answer to these questions is possible, except in the case of the mother of Jesus, we can at least think of these women as representative of the faithful Galilean women who attended the Savior in the Passion narratives. More importantly, they can teach us about coming to Christ and laying hold on his Atonement.

WIDOW OF NAIN

Upon his arrival in Nain, Jesus encountered a funeral procession just exiting the village. Jesus immediately identified the mother of the dead man, knowing that she was a widow and that the dead was her only son. The small village of Nain is located about seven miles southeast of Nazareth, the village where the

Savior grew to manhood. One wonders, was Jesus previously acquainted with the widow's family?

We better appreciate the Lord's instinctive compassion for the widow when we realize that at her husband's death, his estate would have first gone to their son, then after the son's death, to the closest male relative.[1] Without her son, the widow had no means of support and would be left a vulnerable target for exploitation in her society.

Into this poignant funeral scene walked Jesus. He approached the mourning mother and uttered a seemingly impossible command, "Weep not" (Luke 7:13). As the only one with power to give hope and joy in the face of loss, the Savior brings life even when we have not asked. With a touch of his hand and the power of his word, the young man arose, and Christ "delivered him to his mother" (v. 15). Through his atoning sacrifice, the Savior heals broken hearts, restores families, and gives life, even eternal life.

THE WOMAN WHO LOVED MUCH

While a Pharisee named Simon hosted Jesus for dinner, a Galilean woman entered his house carrying an alabaster vial filled with expensive ointment. The scriptures introduce her simply as "a woman in the city, which was a sinner" (Luke 7:37). The Greek verb here is in the imperfect tense, suggesting that she was known from the town and *had been* a sinner but was a sinner no longer.[2]

We do not know her specific sins, only that they were "many" (v. 47). The most common assumption is that she was a prostitute—because she was a woman of means, indicated by her possession of an expensive vial of ointment, and had committed publicly known sins. Just as plausible, however, was that she openly interacted with Gentiles or others considered "unclean." Simon knew her sin because he belonged to the town but expected Jesus to know it by inspiration, if he really were the Prophet,[3] leading us to conclude that one could not deduce her sinful life by her outward appearance.

By teasing out the scriptural text, we may conclude that the woman must have already repented of her sins after a previous encounter with the message of salvation. When she knew that Jesus was at Simon's house, she made preparations to demonstrate her gratitude to him by anointing his feet with the ointment.

Actually being in the presence of Jesus after her repentance may have been even more emotional for the woman than she anticipated. She began to weep when she saw him, and her tears flowed with the ointment. Wiping his feet with her hair rather than a cloth may suggest that her tears were spontaneous and she had no other means to wipe them.[4] Repentant and profoundly humble, she fell at her Savior's feet and kissed them with overwhelming reverence.

By contrast, Simon's self-righteousness bore unspoken witness that he felt that he needed no Redeemer. While the woman wept in humble adoration, Simon silently rebuffed Jesus for allowing a sinner to touch him thus, concluding this was evidence that Jesus was no prophet. Knowing Simon's thoughts, Jesus told him the parable of two debtors, who were both subsequently forgiven by their creditor: "There was a certain creditor which had two debtors: the one owed five hundred pence, and the other fifty. And when they had nothing to pay, he frankly forgave them both. Tell me therefore, which of them will love him most?" (Luke 7:41–42).

In a question pointed to Simon but also meant to be heard by the woman, Jesus asked, "Tell me therefore, which of them will love [the creditor] most?" Simon logically and accurately answered, "I suppose he, to whom he forgave most" (Luke 7:42–43).

Who does love the Savior most? In reality, is it not all those who recognize they have sinned, fallen short, and are forever lost without the atoning blood of Jesus Christ? Bankrupt in spirit and burdened by sin, we come to Christ as unprofitable servants. In such a helpless plight, none of us claims that our sin is merely a fifty-pence problem. Our debt is greater than we can ever repay, time immemorial.

Christ acknowledged the woman's soul-felt repentance by telling Simon, "Her sins, which are many, are forgiven; for she loved much: but to whom little is forgiven, the same loveth little." Then turning directly to the woman, Jesus proclaimed, "Thy sins are forgiven. . . . Thy faith hath saved thee; go in peace" (7:47–48, 50). The Savior's forgiveness of the woman was not a consequence of her love for him at that moment, or of her tears and expensive ointment. Her love for the Savior was a product of his cleansing gift to her. The Apostle John taught, "We love him, because he first loved us" (1 John 4:19). Through her sincere acceptance of the Lord's Atonement, the Galilean woman who loved much teaches us to reverence our Redeemer because of his gift of forgiveness. How can we not, therefore, fall at his feet and manifest our profound love and gratitude to him?

THE MOTHER OF JESUS

Luke next identifies the mother of Jesus among the Galilean women. Presumably still a resident of Nazareth, Jesus' mother appears not to have preferential treatment when her Son came to town. How rarely did she get to talk with him alone or care for him as his mother? Because of the "press" of the crowd, she was often denied such a blessing (Luke 8:19). With his mother near the back of the crowd, Jesus explains that his family expanded beyond his natural family to include all those who "hear the word of God, and do it" (v. 21). A relationship with Christ is not based on lineal descent but rather a willing acceptance of his teachings.

Mary exemplified what the Lord meant by hearing the word of God and doing it from the time the angel appeared to her to announce that she would bear the Son of God. She responded with faith, "Be it unto me according to thy word" (Luke 1:38), not knowing what hardships her discipleship would require of her. Her conviction to do whatever God required echoes the greater words of passion and assurance that her Son cried in the Garden of Gethsemane, "Father, if thou be willing, remove this cup from me: nevertheless not my will, but thine, be done" (Luke 22:42).

When Mary and Joseph took the infant Jesus to the temple to offer a sacrifice according to the law (see Leviticus 12:6–8; Numbers 18:15), the Holy Spirit taught an elderly man named Simeon that this baby was the long-awaited Messiah. When Simeon spoke, however, he did not say that he saw the Messiah but that his eyes were looking upon God's salvation. By revelation, he knew that embodied in this tiny babe were all our hopes and promises for eternity.

Speaking prophetically, Simeon then soberly declared, "This child is set for the fall and rising again of many in Israel; and for a sign which shall be spoken against" (Luke 2:34). Turning to Mary he continued, "a sword shall pierce through thy own soul also that the thoughts of many hearts may be revealed" (v. 35). In other words, because of this child's future mission, many in Israel would be faced with a decision that would lead them either to destruction or to the highest heights. That option for Israel, however, would come at a tremendous cost to Jesus through their rejection of his teachings and Atonement and through his humiliating death on the cross.

Furthermore, this clash of reactions to the Savior would not leave his mother unscathed. Mary's soul would also be wounded during her Son's ministry through divisions within her own family.[5] Discipleship with Jesus Christ transcends family ties. When we are born again, when we "hear the word of God, and do it" (Luke 8:21), Jesus Christ becomes our Father and we become his daughters and his sons. As Mary waited to see Jesus from the back of the Galilean crowd, was her heart pierced when she realized that her Son was not hers alone, but only hers to give to the world?

As a model of discipleship, Mary demonstrates another principle for us. The fact that she was his mother did not reduce her need to "hear the word of God, and do it" any less than us. Mary reminds us that blood lineage is no substitute for the enabling blood of the Atonement. Every one of us, whatever our particular circumstance or family background, is lost without Christ's gift of salvation.

The Daughter of Jairus and the Woman Who Touched the Hem of His Garment

The stories of Jesus raising the daughter of Jairus from the dead and healing the woman with the issue of blood are intertwined in the Luke 8 account. They are therefore most meaningful when viewed together.

Jairus' only daughter, probably his only descendant,[6] was dying at the age of twelve, just as she was coming of age as an adult in her society. Jairus, a ruler of the local synagogue, was forthright and confident yet humbly knelt at Jesus' feet to petition his help. The Lord had more to teach Jairus, however, before going to his home. The girl had died when they finally arrived, perhaps because Jairus needed greater faith in the Savior's power than he possessed at his first petition to Christ. On the way to his home, Jairus saw such faith exemplified in the form of a woman who had been ill for as long as his daughter had lived.

The woman, simply known by her disease, was not dead but was just as good as dead, considering her hopeless circumstance that isolated her from society. The scriptures do not specify the cause of her bleeding, but it is generally considered to have been gynecological in nature. According to the law of Moses, such an illness rendered the woman ritually unclean and anything or anyone that she touched was subsequently unclean (see Leviticus 15:25–31). Her bed, eating utensils, and food she prepared were tainted. Most likely, her family members no longer touched her, and her friends abandoned her long ago.

Luke reports that the woman "spent all her living upon physicians" without a positive resolution (Luke 8:43). This description suggests that she was a wealthy woman at one time—but no more. The woman therefore represents depletion in nearly every way—physically, socially, financially, and emotionally—but not spiritually.[7] In the midst of all her distress, buried in the impossibility of her circumstance, she had one shining hope. With a boldness and determination that must have stretched her weakened body to its limits, the woman crafted a means to access her Savior without anyone's notice. Accustomed to being invisible to society and likely reduced to living near the ground, the woman reached out to touch the border of the Savior's robe as he passed by.

Luke tells us that "immediately" the woman knew she was healed physically (v. 44). The Savior's Atonement, however, extends beyond mending physical pain. He heals broken hearts and sick souls. He makes us whole, spirit and body. At that very moment she knew her body was healed, and Jesus turned to ask, "Who touched me?" (v. 45) The surrounding crowd was oblivious to what was happening. This was between the woman and the Lord. Jesus had a further gift to offer to this woman—but it would require even greater faith on her part. By touching merely the hem of his garment, the woman may have believed that she could be healed without rendering the Savior unclean and without calling down further denunciation and disgust from her neighbors. Now she must stretch her faith to publicly acknowledge what she had done.

After confessing before the townspeople, including a leader of the synagogue, that she was the one who touched him, the Savior called her "daughter" (v. 48). Because of her exceeding faith in him, Jesus openly numbered her among his family and pronounced her whole. She was healed both inwardly and outwardly.

As one of the awestruck bystanders who witnessed this miracle, Jairus suddenly received word, "Thy daughter is dead; trouble not the Master" (v. 49). To him, Jesus said, "Fear not: believe only, and she shall be made whole" (v. 50). How different did these words of assurance sound to Jairus after witnessing this woman's great faith? Was anything too hard for the Lord? When we wholeheartedly come to Christ in our distress, knowing that he is our only hope, he renews, enlarges, and enhances the quality of our lives through his atoning blood.

Mary Magdalene

In all but one of the twelve times that Mary Magdalene is mentioned in the four Gospels, she is alone or the first of a list of women. The sole exception is in John's account of the women at the Crucifixion, when the mother of Jesus is identified first (see John 19:25). The primacy of her name in these lists and the frequency of her mention suggest that Mary Magdalene was a leader among the women. Perhaps that is one reason that Luke specifically named her as one of the Galilean women who ministered to Jesus in his travels and the one out of whom Jesus cast "seven devils" (Luke 8:2).

Mary's ailment involving seven devils may say more about the magnitude of Christ's power to heal than her previous spiritual, emotional, or moral health. The number seven in scripture often connotes completeness and wholeness. In announcing Mary's cure, Luke may simply be confirming that through the power of Christ, Mary was completely healed, she was made whole, or that she was completely liberated from her illness.[8]

In all four Gospels, Mary Magdalene and other Galilean women followed Jesus to Jerusalem where they became active witnesses of his Crucifixion.[9] As sheep without their shepherd, they joined the burial procession to observe where the body was buried and perhaps to observe which burial procedures were completed. Scripture implies that time did not allow for the customary sprinkling of spices and perfumed ointment on the strips of cloth used to wrap around the body prior to burial.[10] Because women were typically the ones who prepared and applied the fragrances, the women of Galilee may have concluded the need to return after the Sabbath for this purpose.

The Gospel narratives as well as traditions that preceded their writing imply that Mary Magdalene and other women from Galilee were the first to discover the empty tomb early on that first Easter morning.[11] Shortly afterward, other disciples witnessed the empty tomb and departed again, filled with their own questions and desires to understand what had occurred, leaving Mary Magdalene alone at the scene. The Gospel of John directs us to follow her quest and subsequent revelation, but no doubt other disciples could testify of their own parallel experience. Mary remained stationed at the empty tomb, seemingly determined not to depart until she learned what had happened to the body of Jesus.

Mary Magdalene did not recognize the Savior when he first appeared and spoke to her, calling her by a nonspecific term, "Woman" (John 20:13). She assumed that he was the gardener. Was her eyesight sufficiently blurred because of her tears, or had Jesus' physical appearance changed to obstruct recognition?

Importantly, Mary did not comprehend the Savior's Resurrection when she discovered the empty tomb or even when she saw the resurrected Christ with her natural eyes. Perhaps the risen Lord wanted her to first know him through her spiritual eyes and ears. In a similar way, the two disciples on the road to Emmaus could not recognize the resurrected Christ because their "eyes were holden" (Luke 24:16). Perhaps the Lord's use of the generic term "woman" can allow each of us, whether man or woman, to put ourselves in Mary's place. Does Mary Magdalene exemplify the Lord's desire for each of us to know him first by the witness of the Spirit?

When the Lord said her name, "Mary," something clicked in her, and her spiritual eyes were opened (John 20:16). Suddenly her encounter with the resurrected Lord had become very personal. In an example of what Jesus taught by way of metaphor in John 10, Mary heard the voice of the Good Shepherd when "he calleth his own sheep by name, and leadeth them out" (John 10:3).

Addressing him as her Master, Mary must have instinctively reached out to him and touched him in some way because the Lord's response, "Touch me not," directed her to discontinue whatever it was that she was doing (John 20:17).[12] Other translations of the Savior's directive are, "Don't cling to me" or "Don't hold me back," which is reflected in the Joseph Smith Translation, "Hold me not." Perhaps Mary anticipated that Jesus had returned to remain with his followers forever and resume their association. In her anxious desire not to lose him again, she wanted to cling to him to keep him there.

He had to leave again, because he had not yet ascended to his Father. One final event in his great victory—returning to the presence of his Father—remained to be accomplished. As he has promised each of us if we come in faith to him and apply his atoning sacrifice in our lives, he will bring us to be "at one" with the Father again.

Many have asked why Mary Magdalene received this remarkable experience. We could just as easily ask, why not? We do not need a unique calling, title, or relationship with the Savior different from any other disciple to receive a spiritual witness. We need a broken heart, faith in him, and an opportunity for him to teach us. If for no other reason, she may have received this blessing simply because she lingered in a quiet spot rather than running off to talk with others. Some of our Church leaders have observed that we would have more spiritual experiences if we didn't talk so much about them.[13] Mary Magdalene teaches us to be still and *learn* that he is God (see Psalm 46:10; D&C 101:16).

CONCLUSION

In large measure, the women of Galilee remain anonymous, thereby putting the focus and importance where it should be—on Jesus Christ. In a personal and very palpable way, each of those women was a recipient and eyewitness of the Savior's sacrifice not only at the end but *during* his mortal ministry. The Atonement was efficacious in their daily lives in Galilee. The enduring discipleship in each of these women bears witness to the retroactive and infinite power of the Atonement.

The women of Galilee also remind us that God loves all his children and is no respecter of persons, that men and women are alike unto him, and that lack of a title or position of authority does not exclude someone from a remarkable spiritual witness. Through the power of the Atonement in experiences that prefigured the Savior's own death and Resurrection, a woman—the widow of Nain—received her only son back to life, and a man—Jairus—witnessed his only daughter die and then live again. And while pondering the meaning of the empty tomb, Mary Magdalene received the visit of the Lord, as did his chosen Apostles.

Finally, the women of Galilee prod us to use our agency wisely to come to him, no matter how hopeless our circumstance or how marginalized we may feel in society. Without fanfare or many words, they reinforce the poignant principle that it is by hearing the Lord's teachings and doing them that we join his family, rather than claiming privilege through notable acquaintance or family ties.

During the weeks following the Savior's Resurrection, "the women, and Mary the mother of Jesus" were numbered among the 120 faithful disciples of Christ (Acts 1:14). When these disciples bore witness "in other tongues" (Acts 2:4) of the "wonderful works of God" (v. 11) on the day of Pentecost, the Apostle Peter explained the phenomenon by citing an ancient prophecy: "And it shall come to pass in the last days, saith God, I will pour out of my Spirit upon all flesh: and your sons and your daughters shall prophesy, . . . and on my servants and on my handmaidens I will pour out in those days of my Spirit; and they shall prophesy" (vv. 17–18; see also Joel 2:28–29).

In the meridian of time, the Church of Jesus Christ commenced after multitudes heard both men and women bear witness of their Redeemer. Our recognition of the breadth of the Savior's power will likewise increase when we hear and appreciate the testimonies of all those who know the Lord—even those whose perspective may be different from our own. When both men and women fervently testify of the stunning reality of the Atonement in their lives, we are all blessed.

NOTES

1. Vasiliki Limberis, "Widow of Nain," in *Women in Scripture*, ed. Carol Meyers (Grand Rapids, MI: Eerdmans, 2000), 439–40.

2. Barbara Reid, *Choosing the Better Part? Women in the Gospel of Luke* (Collegeville, MN: Liturgical Press, 1996), 113.

3. Joseph A. Fitzmyer, *The Gospel According to Luke I–IX*, Anchor Bible, vol. 28 (New York: Doubleday, 1981), 689.

4. I. Howard Marshall, *Commentary on Luke*, New International Greek Testament Commentary (Grand Rapids, MI: Eerdmans, 1978), 308–9.

5. Kenneth L. Barker and John R. Kohlengerger III, *The Expositor's Bible Commentary—Abridged Edition: New Testament* (Grand Rapids, MI: Zondervan, 1994), 219–20; Raymond E. Brown, Karl P. Donfried, Joseph A. Fitzmyer, and John Reumann, *Mary in the New Testament* (Philadelphia: Fortress Press, 1978), 154–57; Fitzmyer, *The Gospel According to Luke*, 429–30.

6. Fitzmyer, *The Gospel According to Luke*, 745.

7. Reid, *Choosing the Better Part?* 139.

8. Reid, *Choosing the Better Part?* 126.

9. Joseph A. Fitzmyer, *The Gospel According to Luke X–XXIV*, Anchor Bible, vol. 28A (New York: Doubleday, 1985), 1521.

10. F. F. Bruce, *The Gospel of John* (Grand Rapids, MI: Eerdmans, 1983), 379.

11. See Matthew 28:1–6; Mark 16:1–6; Luke 23:55–24:10. In John 20:1, Mary Magdalene alone discovers the empty tomb. In her report to the Apostles in the following verse, however, she states, "we" do not know where he is, implying that others accompanied her in making this initial discovery, as the synoptic Gospels

report; see also Raymond E. Brown, *The Gospel According to John XIII–XXI*, Anchor Bible, vol. 29A (New York: Doubleday, 1970), 977–78, 1001. Rather than suggesting that the women returned to anoint the body with fragrances, the *Gospel of Peter* posits that they came to appropriately "weep and lament" for the loss of a loved one, as "women are wont to do for those beloved of them who die" (vv. 50–52; in W. Schneemelcher, ed., Robert McL. Wilson, trans., *New Testament Apocrypha* [Louisville, KY: John Knox, 1991], 1:225).

12. Brown, *The Gospel According to John XIII–XXI*, 992; Bruce, *The Gospel of John*, 389–90.

13. Neal A. Maxwell, quoting Marion G. Romney, in "Called to Serve," *BYU 1993–94 Devotional and Fireside Speeches* (Provo, UT: Brigham Young University, 1994), 137.

Minerva K. Teichert, *Rescue of the Lost Lamb*,
© Intellectual Reserve, Inc.

MY PORTRAIT OF JESUS: A WORK IN PROGRESS

Bonnie D. Parkin

Maybe because I love to garden, Easter is a particularly wondrous time for me. I marvel at how, after five months of blizzards and icicles, when colors are not much more than blue and gray, the earth can produce brilliant yellow crocuses, dancing daffodils, and vibrant red tulips. It seems impossible that life can suddenly spring forth from winter's barrenness. As I stand over my garden beds, warmed by the long-absent sun, I am overwhelmed by the way in which all things witness there is a Supreme Creator (see Alma 30:44).

For three years, my husband, Jim, and I lived in England while he served as president of the England London South Mission. Our lives were blessed beyond expectation serving with

---

Bonnie D. Parkin *is a former Relief Society general president.*

missionaries from around the world and with wonderful British Saints. One evening we had invited all the stake mission presidents to the mission home. One of them related a recent experience I have been unable to forget. While it raises some disconcerting questions about society, it has also caused me to ask some questions of myself. Here is his story.

He had gone to a jewelry store to purchase a gift for his wife. The woman in front of him indicated to the jeweler she was looking for something specific. She walked from glass case to glass case. The jeweler asked if he could help her find anything. She said she wanted to see the cross necklaces. So the jeweler took her over to the case with the crosses. He showed her several trays of necklaces, but she impatiently said no to each of them. Finally, in frustration, she said, "No, I'm looking for a cross with the little man on it."

I could not believe it: Here was a woman in the late twentieth century who did not know that the man on the cross was her Savior and—if she knew who Christ was at all—did not know he had been crucified for *her*. Or why. Or that he had risen on the third day. Or that, most importantly, her hope for eternal life depended on him. These thoughts led me to reflect on what *I* knew about Jesus.

Of all times of year, when new life bursts into being, is there a more important time to know Jesus than at Easter?

Recently my granddaughter Ruby came to visit us. She told me about a family home evening lesson where her dad shared an experience. Her father had attended a business meeting. It was a high-stakes negotiation; the discussions had become heated and contentious. As tensions rose, one of the negotiators repeatedly took the Lord's name in vain. Finally, Ruby's dad stood and said, "Stop—please don't use Christ's name like that. He is my Savior." There was an embarrassed silence. When the meeting continued, the mood was subdued, more productive. Afterward, this chief negotiator approached my son and apologized for his insensitivity. Hearing how her father valued the sacredness of the Savior's name and had defended him left as lasting an impression on Ruby and her siblings as it did on me. I pray this story will always remind my grandchildren of the sacredness of the Savior's name and help them control their own expressions.

Adlai Stevenson is said to have told a story of two girls who were drawing pictures. The first little girl said, "What is it you are drawing?" "Why, I'm drawing a picture of Jesus," answered the other. "How can you?" responded the first. "Nobody knows what Jesus looks like." "Well," said the other girl, "that's 'cause I haven't finished my picture yet!"

Jesus asked his disciples, "Whom say ye that I am?" (Mark 8:29). I want to be able to answer his question with an answer which reflects that *I know* who he is. And yet, like that little girl, my picture of Jesus is still in progress. Small parts of this portrait are beautifully rendered with luminous highlights and rich, detailed shadows, but others remain blurs—or even blank spots—on the canvas.

The best artists are those who capture through color, light, shadow, and gesture, the essence of their subject. The best portraits allow us to see not only the outside of another person—the style of their clothing, the color of their hair, and so on—but they allow us to see *inside* another person. In other words, who they *are*. They create a relationship—a visual conversation—between the subject and us. Such portraits allow us to feel that we know the subject and that the artist does as well.

I have read that many great artists, before ever picking up a brush, spend time getting to know their subjects by reading about them and spending time with them in their day-to-day lives. They ask questions and then listen closely to the answers. They visit the subjects' homes and families. Only when artists feel they really know their subjects do they begin to paint. Then, somehow, the inner character of the subjects is brought to the surface.

Creating a portrait with such illuminating qualities requires great dedication from the painter, even more so in attempting a portrait of the Savior. Yet that is what I want my portrait of Jesus to be. I want its viewers, especially my children and grandchildren, not only to know Jesus but to know that I know him.

SEEKING AND KNOWING JESUS

"And now I would commend you," wrote Moroni, "to seek this Jesus of whom the prophets and apostles have written." Why did Moroni give us such a commandment? So "that the grace of God the Father, and also the Lord Jesus Christ, and the Holy Ghost, which beareth record of them, may be and abide in [us] forever" (Ether 12:41). In other words, that we "might know . . . the only true God, and Jesus Christ, whom [he] hast sent" (John 17:3). Such knowledge is eternal life. Oh how I want to know him better!

Is there someone in your life who, as you have come to know them intimately—how they act, how they treat others, how they feel about you—has revealed hidden brushstrokes that inspired you to reach deeper into yourself and emulate them? My life has been blessed with countless such people. In my mind's eye, I can see their faces. They have been divinely placed around me as family, ward members, Church leaders, neighbors, and friends—both Latter-day Saints and non–Latter-day Saints. They are the people around the world whom I have been so blessed to visit with through the years; such associations bring a frequent response, the desire to improve. I see purity, obedience, service, endurance, reverence, faith, hope, charity. My heart is enriched, my soul expanded by these connections across the globe. In my times of weakness or discouragement, joy and celebration, I think of those I know and have known, and I am inspired to become a little more like them.

I wonder if this same effect is why we are commanded to seek and come to know Jesus—not because he wants an everlasting, adoring fan club. Like all his commandments, the timeless prophetic pleadings to come know him is for *us*. As we learn about him and learn who he is, we strive to become more like him.

As the Prophet Joseph Smith taught, "Remember . . . that He has called you unto holiness; and . . . to be like Him in purity." How can we become like him if we do not know him?[1]

When I was a young mother with small children, there came a time when I felt a deep yearning to know Jesus Christ. In an effort to deepen my knowledge of and acquaintance with him, my personal study focused on Elder James E. Talmage's book *Jesus the Christ*. I shall never forget when I read these words: "[Jesus'] development was unretarded by the dragging weight of sin; He loved and obeyed the truth and therefore was free."[2]

What an insight into Jesus' character! As I pondered this short sentence, I realized that I was developing and wanted unretarded growth, that I wanted freedom from the dragging weight of sin. How could I do that? Through obedience to truth. Just like Jesus. For years, Elder Talmage's words found a prominent place under a magnet on our refrigerator door. This knowledge spurred my feelings to action. I vividly recall a testimony meeting shortly after discovering this insight. The Spirit overcame me with an enormous need to stand and testify of Jesus. And as I did, my knowledge of him deepened and expanded; I came to know him just a little bit better.

Looking back, I realize my acquaintance with the Savior has come from countless influences. They are diverse in nature yet, when combined, serve to help me create a more complete portrait of Jesus. One such influence came early in my youth.

As a young girl, I was blessed by an aunt I never met. My dear mother had a sister, Rachel, who was two years younger. They were very close, even sharing the same birthday: May first. When Mother talked about Aunt Rachel, it was with great fondness and love. She told of sharing a bed, playing together, and swimming in the Idaho canals—Aunt Rachel loved to swim. She said Rachel was the best English student in her high school and spoke proudly of her wonderful poems and stories. Besides excelling in her studies, Aunt Rachel was blessed with a lovely sense of color and skillful hands that could crochet just about anything.

After high school, Rachel moved to San Francisco. She stayed with a widowed aunt who lived alone. She studied at Mount Zion Hospital to become a registered nurse and eventually passed her boards with a perfect score. She was asked to be the superintendent of student nurses at the French Hospital. Mother and her family were so proud of Aunt Rachel and all her accomplishments. Then, one day they received word that Aunt

Rachel had been swimming in the San Francisco Bay and had drowned. She was only twenty-two.

Mother missed Aunt Rachel deeply. So even though we had never met Aunt Rachel, Mother wanted us to somehow know this special aunt and to love her. In our home was a beautiful afghan that Aunt Rachel had crocheted. I can still see it—warm autumn colors of browns, oranges, yellows, and reds. When we were sick, mother would say, "Let's put Aunt Rachel's arms around you." Then she'd snuggle us up in that afghan and say, "You will feel better soon." It always worked. Even though I had only seen pictures of Aunt Rachel, oh how I loved her! Why? Because when I was in need, I had felt her arms around me.

Loving Aunt Rachel grew naturally out of learning about her. Her afghan was something tangible that I could wrap around me. When I was cold it warmed me, but not just physically. It also provided inner warmth because I knew somehow that she loved me. That afghan helped me realize how, more than anything else, feelings help us truly know and love someone—know them well enough that we might be able to paint them.

Aunt Rachel's afghan is an unlikely source for a connection to Christ. I have had no tangible interaction with Jesus, no afghan to wrap around me. Yet in my hours of need, my times of sickness, my discouragements and disappointments, I have felt his arms around me, wrapping me in everlasting love. "Our Redeemer took upon Himself all the sins, pains, infirmities, and sicknesses of all who have ever lived and will ever live."[3] As Alma said to his son Helaman, "I have been supported under trials and troubles of every kind, yea, and in all manner of afflictions; yea, God has delivered me from prison, and from bonds, and from death; yea, and I do put my trust in him, and he will still deliver me" (Alma 36:27). It is through such feelings—love and rescue, safety and salvation—that I have best come to know Jesus.

So many of these feelings have come from the scriptures— accounts from those who knew Jesus and the ways their interactions with him affected them. Over and over people describe how being with him made them feel.

I think of the two disciples walking to Emmaus after the Crucifixion. As they journeyed, they talked sadly about the events of the past three days, and Jesus approached and joined them, unrecognized. They discussed the events of Jesus' death, and he spoke to them about the gospel, citing scripture after scripture to put everything in perspective. As they were about to part ways, they pleaded with him to stay a little longer. Yet they did not recognize him until after he had broken bread with them and then vanished from their midst. At that point they said to each other, "Did not our heart burn within us, while he talked with us by the way, and while he opened to us the scriptures?" (Luke 24:32). I love the description that their hearts burned within them. They were changed by the experience, blessed with a deepened understanding and great joy—joy so great they immediately sought to share it with others (see Luke 24:33–52).

My heart has burned within me as I have testified that Jesus is my Savior. He speaks heart to heart, in a way that leaves no doubt as to how he feels about me: he loves me and counts me his. Lehi tasted of the fruit of the tree of life, which is the love of God (see 1 Nephi 11:22). It "filled [his] soul with exceedingly great joy" and made him "desirous that [his] family should partake of it also; for [he] knew that it was desirable above all other fruit" (1 Nephi 8:12). Like Lehi, I too have tasted of this fruit. I testify that it is "the most desirable above all things . . . and the most joyous to the soul" (1 Nephi 11:22–23). Because I have tasted of this fruit, I have strived to speak heart to heart, to inspire my sisters and brothers to feel the sweet love of the Lord in their lives. I have endeavored, through my testimony and my service, to be an extension of his loving feelings. And as I have reached out to others to the best of my abilities, I have felt his love again. This celestial cycle has validated King Benjamin's words that I am forever in the Lord's debt (see Mosiah 2:23–24). This unfailing generosity teaches me to go and do likewise.

My painting of Jesus is not static—he is not sitting. Rather, he is standing, arms outstretched, beckoning me. As the Lord has spoken to my heart, I have learned the eternal significance of belonging: he desperately wants us to belong—to him and to each other. When I have felt pains of isolation or have witnessed the pain of others who feel the same, I have pictured this image of the Savior with his arms extended. His gentle words pierce the loneliness: "Come unto me, all ye that labour and are heavy laden, and I will give you rest" (Matthew 11:28). This tender image calls me to extend my own arms to those who feel excluded so that they might be included. It causes me to see the Savior in others who step forward and do the same for me. I experience such extensions of lifting love from Saints—especially my sisters—around the world.

When I was called to serve in the Relief Society, the overwhelming inspiration was to testify to each sister around the globe that the Lord knows them and loves them. In wanting women to feel the love of the Lord in their lives, I felt I needed to better understand how Jesus felt about women. One of my early insights came from President Boyd K. Packer, but not in the way you might guess. As you can imagine, my new calling was somewhat overwhelming. I went to President Packer to seek his counsel. When I sat down in his office, he did not launch into a lecture on how to run Relief Society. He did not tell me how to make beautiful centerpieces. Instead, he listened. From then on, I knew I could count on him to listen to my thoughts, then share his perspective and counsel. As I would leave his office, he would say, "My door is always open to you." President Packer is a special witness of Christ, so was it any surprise that he listened to women?

My presidency and I felt impressed to use the story of Mary and Martha as the focus of one of the general Relief Society meetings. This story revolves around Jesus' association with two women; it illustrates how he values us. As we prepared for the meeting by studying this and other scriptures, we soon discovered that not only did Jesus make a place for women, he was an ennobler of women.

In *Jesus the Christ*, Elder Talmage spoke of "the little sisterhood of faithful women who . . . ministered to Jesus in Galilee and . . . followed him thence to Jerusalem and to Calvary." He referred to these special women as Jesus' "other disciples."[4]

To emphasize the Savior's feeling toward women, Elder Talmage quotes Cunningham Geikie, who wrote that Jesus "swept away for ever from His Society the conception of woman as a mere toy or slave of man, and based true relations of the sexes on the eternal foundation of truth, right, honor, and love. To ennoble the House and the Family by raising woman to her true position was essential to the future stability of His Kingdom, as one of purity and spiritual worth. . . . He proclaimed the equal rights of woman and man within the limits of the family, and, in this, gave their charter of nobility to the mothers of the world. For her nobler position in the Christian era, compared with that granted her in antiquity, woman is indebted to Jesus Christ."[5] I testify that this is true.

Could anything speak more powerfully to this than the fact that, following his Resurrection, a *woman*, Mary Magdalene, "was given the honor of being the first among mortals to behold a resurrected Soul, and that Soul, the Lord Jesus"?[6] Jesus asked her, "Woman, why weepest thou? whom seekest thou?" And she, supposing him to be the gardener, said, "Sir, if thou have borne him hence, tell me where thou hast laid him." Then Jesus called her gently by name, "Mary." She undoubtedly recognized the great love in his voice and turned to him, responding, "Master" (John 20:15–16).

I recall leaving for our mission to England. Sitting among all those strangers on the airplane, I realized that for the next three years I would not be "Bonnie" but would be known only by the name on my tag: Sister Parkin. I confess this made me a little sad. I glanced down at my name tag. Below "Sister Parkin" I saw another name: Jesus Christ. My heart rejoiced. I was honored to share that name tag with my Savior. If nobody else knew I was Bonnie, He did. He knew Mary, and called her by name, and He knew me, and He called me. I was thrilled to respond and call him Master. After arriving in London, we called home to check on our family. Our three-year-old grandson James asked, "Grandmother, do you work for Jesus?" Humbled, I stopped a moment, then said, "Yes, James. I do work for Jesus."

Nobody "works for Jesus" better than his dear prophet. Like Jesus, President Hinckley valued women. I recall a general welfare meeting with the First Presidency, members of the Twelve, and other General Authorities. The Relief Society general presidency was asked to make a presentation. My counselors, Kathy Hughes and Anne Pingree, and I felt inspired to teach a principle as we did when training Relief Society leaders, which included asking questions and expecting responses. Such an approach was unusual for the welfare meeting. As expected, the Brethren were initially surprised with this approach. But they soon participated enthusiastically.

After the meeting, President Hinckley walked into his office and said to his secretary, Don Staheli, "Don, don't let me forget. Don't let me forget."

"Forget what, President?" asked Brother Staheli.

President Hinckley smiled thoughtfully, then said, "Today we were taught by the women of the Church and we were no less for it."

At the next general conference, President Hinckley said: "I witnessed a very interesting thing the other day. The General Authorities were in a meeting, and the presidency of the Relief Society were there with us. These able women stood in our council room and shared with us principles of welfare and of helping those who are in distress. Our stature as officers of this Church was not diminished by what they did. Our capacities to serve were increased."[7] What a significant moment! I learned through Jesus' prophet how he felt about the women of the Church.

Paintings are often layered with multiple meanings. In my painting, Jesus' outstretched arms say more to me than inclusion—they also communicate constant loyalty. "He is not ashamed to call [me sister]" (Hebrews 2:11).

A few months ago, the father of a dear friend passed away. His first wife had died many years before, and he had remarried.

In preparing for the funeral, my friend's stepmother requested that the funeral be a celebration of her husband's life rather than a religious service. This must have been difficult for the children, as they were all active members of the Church. My friend was torn as to what to do: she wanted to honor her stepmother's request, but she also felt prompted to testify of Christ—something she often does. Throughout the funeral service, she kept praying that she would do the right thing. Near the end of the service when she finally stood to speak, my friend spoke of her father and the important lessons he had taught her in life. Then, acting upon the strong, undeniable impression she had received while preparing her talk, she testified of Jesus Christ and his Atonement. The words were few, but they were filled with power. She said, "I *know* that because of the Savior's Atonement, one day there will be a joyous reunion with my father and other loved ones." Then she closed her talk in the name of Jesus Christ. As she did so, the Spirit filled the room, ratifying her words. Tears rolled down my cheeks and, I am sure, the cheeks of others. I was strengthened by my dear friend's courageous testimony.

The good news of Easter helps me understand my Savior in a broader, eternal perspective. During a visit to President Hinckley's office, I asked him, "How are you doing, President?" "I'm lonely," he said. He told me how the night before he had been reading the Wilford Woodruff study guide that was to come out the next year. He paused, then, referring to his deceased wife, Marjorie, said, "I don't know if I dreamed it or if I heard her voice, but she said, 'I'm having a grand time. Wish you were here.'" It was not long after that that President Hinckley joined his wife in what was surely a joyous reunion. Now, united once more, I am sure they are having a grand time together. That is the good news of Easter. Who would provide for such reunions but an elder brother willing to sacrifice his life for ours?

"The testimony of our Lord's rising from the dead is not founded on written pages," wrote James E. Talmage. "To him who seeks in faith and sincerity shall be given an individual conviction which shall enable him to reverently confess as exclaimed the enlightened apostle of old: 'Thou art the Christ, the Son of the living God.' Jesus, who is God the Son, is not dead. 'I know that my Redeemer liveth.'"[8]

The Relief Society motto proclaims, "Charity never faileth." Charity, says Mormon, "is the pure love of Christ." I have often wondered if this means it is the love Jesus has for us or if it is the love we have for Jesus, or if it is both. Upon being called to serve in the Relief Society, I felt a special charge to communicate the Lord's love for each sister around the globe and to testify of that unfailing love. So I began a yearlong study about charity. We studied it as a presidency and as a board. We pondered on and discussed each attribute. I love the definition of the Lord's love: "Charity suffereth long, and is kind, and envieth not, and is not puffed up, seeketh not her own, is not easily provoked, thinketh no evil, and rejoiceth not in iniquity but rejoiceth in the truth, beareth all things, believeth all things, hopeth all things, endureth all things. . . . Wherefore, cleave unto charity, which is the greatest of all, for all things must fail—but charity is the pure love of Christ, and it endureth forever" (Moroni 7:45–47).

That description of the pure love of Christ speaks volumes about who Jesus is. It is specific and concrete; it is deceptively simple. It might be discouraging if not for my painting of Jesus and his outstretched arms, beckoning, cheering, buoying. In that description, I see who my Savior is and who I can be. If Jesus can be kind to his captors, I can be kind to all. If Jesus can forgive his crucifiers, I can forgive everyone. If Jesus can love me in spite of all of my shortcomings, I can do likewise.

I do not know if there is a more poignant or poetic depiction of Jesus than these words of Isaiah: "He is despised and rejected of men; a man of sorrows, and acquainted with grief: and we hid as it were our faces from him; he was despised, and we esteemed him not. Surely he hath borne our griefs, and carried our sorrows: yet we did esteem him stricken, smitten of God, and afflicted. But he was wounded for our transgressions, he was bruised for our iniquities: the chastisement of our peace was upon him; and with his stripes we are healed" (Isaiah 53:3–5).

Only eighty-two words, yet Isaiah's insights on Jesus and our relationship with him are stunning. They invoke pity, shame, humility, empathy, gratitude. I can scarcely take in the final six words: "with his stripes we are healed." I don't understand how that works! Nor do I fully understand why he would be wounded for my transgressions or bruised for my iniquities.

I paraphrase these words by Joseph Smith as I reflect on my painting of the Savior: "When [I] reflect upon the holiness and perfections of [my] great Master, who has opened a way whereby [I] may come unto him, even by the sacrifice of himself, *[my] heart melt[s] within [me] for his condescension.*"[9]

I love the image-rich lyrics of the hymn "Jesus, the Very Thought of Thee."[10]

> Jesus, the very thought of thee
> With sweetness fills my breast;
> But sweeter far thy face to see
> And in thy presence rest.

Nor voice can sing, nor heart can frame,
Nor can the mem'ry find
A sweeter sound than thy blest name,
O Savior of mankind!

O hope of ev'ry contrite heart,
O joy of all the meek,
To those who fall, how kind thou art!
How good to those who seek!

Jesus, our only joy be thou,
As thou our prize wilt be;
Jesus, be thou our glory now,
And thru eternity.

There is no artist capable of capturing the complete essence of Jesus. For how can a painting even begin to capture such mercy, such love, such devotion? How can paint on canvas contain an eternal being of such majesty as to command the respect of all things in the heavens and the earth?

I have come to the realization that my best portrait of Jesus will not be rendered on a figurative canvas. Rather, it will be created in who I become—a person who has "received his image in [my] countenance" (Alma 5:14). My countenance, like all skillful portraits, will capture the essence of who I am. But if this is to be, I cannot be the artist. For there is only one artist capable of producing such a grand work of art. He is the master painter.

Because we have sought him and know him and have allowed him to change us, we will be like him. His image will shine through us. Could anything be sweeter or more humbling or more joyous than not only to see Jesus in our countenances but to feel His character through every fiber of our beings?

Like the magnificence of spring flowers bursting from winter's bleakness, I love the hope Moroni extends us near the end of the Book of Mormon: "Pray unto the Father with all the energy of heart, that ye may be filled with this love, which he hath bestowed upon all who are true followers of his Son, Jesus Christ; that ye may become the [children] of God; that when he shall appear *we shall be like him, for we shall see him as he is*; that we may have this hope; that we may be purified even as he is pure" (Moroni 7:48; emphasis added).

I testify that Jesus is the Christ. He is my Savior, my Lord, my God. I pray that when he appears I shall see him as he is and shall be like him. As comforting as Aunt Rachel's afghan was to me as a child, I, like President Faust, "long for the ultimate blessing of the Atonement—to become one with Him, to be in His divine presence, to be called individually by name as He warmly welcomes us home with a radiant smile, beckoning us with open arms to be enfolded in His boundless love."[11]

NOTES

1. "The Elders of the Church in Kirtland, to Their Brethren Abroad," *Evening and Morning Star*, March 1834, 142.

2. James E. Talmage, *Jesus the Christ* (Salt Lake City: Deseret Book, 1977), 112.

3. James E. Faust, "The Atonement: Our Greatest Hope," *Ensign*, November 2001, 19.

4. Talmage, *Jesus the Christ*, 700.

5. Cunningham Geikie, *Life and Words of Christ* (London: Henry S. King, 1877), 2:349, as quoted in Talmage, *Jesus the Christ*, 484.

6. Talmage, *Jesus the Christ*, 681.

7. Gordon B. Hinckley, "The Women in Our Lives," in Conference Report, October 2004, 87.

8. Talmage, *Jesus the Christ*, 699.

9. *Teachings of Presidents of the Church: Joseph Smith* (Salt Lake City: The Church of Jesus Christ of Latter-day Saints, 2007), 53–54.

10. Bernard of Clairvaux, "Jesus, the Very Thought of Thee," *Hymns* (Salt Lake City: The Church of Jesus Christ of Latter-day Saints, 1985), no. 141.

11. Faust, "The Atonement: Our Greatest Hope," 20.

Ron Richmond, *Exchange No. 8*,
Brigham Young University Museum of Art.

JESUS' ATONEMENT FORETOLD THROUGH HIS BIRTH

Lynne Hilton Wilson

Easter is the zenith of all Christian doctrine and experience. Much scripture points to this great event. Even the chronicles of the Lord's birth prefigure Easter. In both plain and intricate ways, the events recorded in Matthew's and Luke's first two chapters masterfully foreshadow the Lord's rejection, Passion, Atonement, death, and Resurrection.[1] Their stories are filled with meaning and prophecy. They tell a story within a story. Wicked Herod and righteous Zacharias, the Virgin Mary and upright Joseph, the shepherds and wise men—all these individuals and their stories reveal a testimony of Jesus' divinity and Atonement. But our familiarity with the nativity narratives sometimes causes us to miss the deeper witness of the Atonement, of which the authors bear record. A typological

Lynne Hilton Wilson *is a PhD candidate in theology at Marquette University and an institute teacher at Stanford Institute of Religion.*

examination of the nativity accounts adds a deeper appreciation of Jesus' role as the atoning Savior and Redeemer. Connections between the beginning and ending of the Lord's life bear witness of his divine mission and are portrayed historically, linguistically, typologically, and prophetically. This paper offers examples of themes and words from the beginning of Matthew's and Luke's Gospels that reflect events associated with Jesus' atoning sacrifice.

KING OF KINGS VERSUS KINGS OF MEN

The political setting of Jesus' birth contrasts the disparity between mortal rulers and the King of Kings. Luke identified by name Caesar Augustus (27 BC–AD 14), who ruled at the time of Jesus' birth. Augustus was known as the emperor who pacified the world. His victories put an end to the violent Roman wars, and he was labeled "Savior of the Whole World."[2] His birthday was embraced as the beginning of the New Year. In addition, his adopted father, Julius Caesar, had been posthumously proclaimed a god by the senate in 42 BC, so Augustus used the paradoxical title "son of god" as part of his official nomenclature on coins and inscriptions.[3] Luke 2:1 introduces Augustus and accentuates the ironies between the emperor's life and Jesus' nativity. It was not accidental that Luke's description of Jesus' birth, life, and death present a challenge to this imperial Roman propaganda. Luke's Gospel powerfully proclaims that Jesus, not Caesar, brought real peace to the world. In describing the first Christmas and Easter, Luke testifies that Jesus, not Caesar, is the "Son of God" (Luke 1:35; 22:70).

The title "king" is used by both Herods, at the beginning and end of Jesus' life (see Matthew 2:1; Mark 6:22). Both Herods attack Jesus, who receives the same title—respectfully from the wise men and spitefully from the soldiers and Pilate (see Matthew 2:2; 27:29, 37). Right from the start of his Gospel, Matthew draws attention to this political irony with Herod the Great's title, "King of the Jews" (Matthew 2:2). Josephus describes Herod the Great as pathologically jealous and preoccupied with usurpers.[4] Herod probably felt personally challenged by the wise men's announcement of another "King of the Jews." This scene in Matthew begins the political drama of Jesus' mortal life. It is not complete until his Crucifixion, when Pilate writes the title "King of the Jews" for Jesus' cross (see Matthew 27:37; Mark 15:26; Luke 23:38; John 19:19).

Matthew begins his Gospel with a Jewish leader questioning Jesus' title as "King of the Jews" and ends with other leaders questioning the same title: "The governor asked him, saying, Art thou the King of the Jews? . . . and they bowed the knee before him, and mocked him, saying, Hail, King of the Jews!" (Matthew 27:11, 29; see also Matthew 27:42).

Matthew's use of Jesus' royal title in the nativity narrative is echoed in his Passion account. The wise men ask King Herod for information about the new "King of the Jews" (Matthew 2:2). Two verses later, King Herod uses a different royal title when he demands information from the chief priests and scribes about "where *Christ* should be born" (Matthew 2:4; emphasis added). The same two titles are interchanged in Matthew when the chief priest demands, "Tell us whether thou be the Christ" (Matthew 26:63). Yet the Romans crucify him as "King of the Jews" (Matthew 27:37). Further, the wise men worshipped the Christ child as King of Kings: "When they were come into the house, they saw the young child with Mary his mother, and fell down, and worshipped him" (Matthew 2:11). Both birth narratives and the Passion narrative witness of Jesus' identity as a king.

"BOOK OF THE *GENESIS* OF JESUS CHRIST"[5]

Both Matthew's and Luke's narratives use Joseph's genealogy to testify of Jesus' mission (see Matthew 1:1–17; Luke 3:23–38).[6] The former testifies of Jesus' mission as the messianic son of David, and the latter, as the Son of God. Matthew uses Joseph's genealogy to prove that "Jesus Christ [is] the son of David" (1:1) by organizing the names around the number fourteen (the numeric value of the Hebrew letters in David's name, *dwd*).[7] With names and numbers, Matthew witnesses that Jesus is a descendant of King David and that he thus fulfilled the messianic prophecies (see Matthew 1:17; Genesis 49:10). In Matthew's Gospel, two blind men, a woman from Canaan, and the multitude on Palm Sunday herald, "Hosanna to the Son of David: Blessed is he that cometh in the name of the Lord" (Matthew 21:9; also see 9:27; 15:22; 20:30–31; 21:15). Matthew uses the title "Son of David" to connect Jesus' birth and mission together by testifying of his role as the Davidic Messiah.

Luke's genealogy is masterfully constructed around the number seven—symbolizing completeness or perfection.[8] The genealogy immediately follows Jesus' baptism, where the voice of the Father proclaims, "Thou art my beloved Son," and Luke then adds a second witness through genealogy to trace Jesus back as "a Son of God" (Luke 3:22, 38). Luke's underlying message proclaims that Jesus came from the ultimate source of perfection,

"God"—the seventy-seventh name.[9] Luke's Gospel leaves no question as to whose son Jesus was. The author even pauses in his introduction to assure his audience that Joseph was only the "supposed" paternity (Luke 3:23). The title "Son of God" is scattered through all the Gospels, which serves as a recurring testimony of Jesus' divinity. Ironically it was the same title that would bring him his death sentence (John 19:7; Luke 22:70). Outside of Luke's Gospel, the last voice to testify of this in Jesus' mortality comes from the Gentile centurion at the foot of Jesus' cross: "Truly this man was the Son of God" (Mark 15:39).

"The Angel of the Lord Came upon Them"

Angelic visitations fill the infancy and Passion accounts.[10] In Matthew's Gospel, Joseph has four dreams in which the "angel of the Lord" directs him.[11] This term reflects a Hebrew construct, *mal'ak yhwh* or "messenger of Jehovah." The phrase "angel of the Lord" is not mentioned again in Matthew's Gospel until the morning of the Lord's Resurrection. "Behold there was a great earthquake: for the *angel of the Lord* descended from heaven, and came and rolled back the stone from the door, and sat upon it" (Matthew 28:2; emphasis added). And a few verses later, the same angel of the Lord speaks to the women at the tomb (see Matthew 28:5–7).

In Luke's infancy narrative, the angel Gabriel visits Zacharias in the temple sanctuary (see Luke 1:11–20) and Mary in Nazareth (see Luke 1:26–38).[12] An unnamed angel visits the shepherds in the fields followed by a heavenly host proclaiming, "Glory to God in the highest, and on earth peace" (Luke 2:14). Luke seems to draw this angelic herald together with the disciples' testimony thirty-three years later on Palm Sunday: "Peace in heaven, and glory in the highest" (Luke 19:38). Outside of the infancy chapters, Luke records only one other appearance of an angel, thus suggesting a link between the birth and Passion narratives; while Jesus was suffering in the Garden of Gethsemane, "there appeared an angel unto him from heaven, strengthening him. And being in an agony he prayed more earnestly: and his sweat was as it were great drops of blood falling down to the ground" (Luke 22:43–44). At the Annunciation, birth of Christ, suffering in Gethsemane, and rising from the tomb, angels are reported as watching, protecting, and preparing the way for Jesus to fulfill his mission as our Savior and King.

"BEHOLD THE HANDMAID OF THE LORD"

The theme of obedient submissive service in Mary's and Simeon's lives is magnified to a divine degree in the life of Mary's Son. In the first chapter of Luke, Mary acquiesces herself to the angel Gabriel as "the handmaid of the Lord" (Luke 1:38). The Greek word *doulê* means both slave and servant.[13] Submissiveness was well understood in the Roman world, where one-third of the population was slaves. The word carried a powerful message. Luke chooses a masculine form of the word *doulos* a chapter later when Simeon identifies himself as a servant of the Lord: "Lord, now lettest thou thy servant depart in peace" (Luke 2:29; emphasis added). Simeon's poem foretells of Jesus' submitting to the role of the Suffering Servant, forming another link between the birth and death accounts (see Luke 2:34–35).[14] Jesus identified himself as a servant during his last week of life while preaching at the temple: "He that is greatest among you shall be your servant" (Matthew 23:11). The word used by Matthew is *diako-nos*, meaning "servant of a king."[15] Jesus fully served his Father: "I seek not mine own will, but the will of the Father which hath sent me" (John 5:30). At the Last Supper, he acknowledges, "I have kept my Father's commandments" (John 15:10); and in the Garden of Gethsemane, "Father, . . . not my will, but thine, be done" (Luke 22:42; also Matthew 26:39; Mark 14:36). The theme of submissiveness is introduced in the birth narratives and reflected at the close of Jesus' life.

"THE SON OF THE HIGHEST"

Jesus is identified unequivocally as having a divine Father in the nativity and death accounts. In the birth chapters, it is stated boldly and without question (see Matthew 1:20–25; 2:2; Luke 1:32, 35, 42–45; 2:11). It is also one of the few points that Matthew and Luke share in their birth accounts. Jesus was not Joseph's literal son but the Son of God. Matthew records the angel of the Lord appearing to his main character and saying, "Joseph, thou son of David, fear not to take unto thee Mary thy wife: for that which is conceived in her is of the Holy Ghost" (Matthew 1:20). Likewise in Luke, the angel appears to Mary, Luke's principal character, and says, "The Holy Ghost shall come upon thee, and the power of the Highest shall overshadow thee: therefore also that holy thing which shall be born of thee shall be called the Son of God" (Luke 1:35).[16] The witnesses of Jesus' divine birth did not fully comprehend his mission, however. In Luke's Passion narrative, Jesus' claim as the Son of God did not escape the fury of Jewish leaders, who indicted him for making this blasphemous assertion (see Luke 22:70–71).

Jesus consistently referred to God as his Father. For example, in Gethsemane he prayed, "Abba, Father, . . . take away this cup from me: nevertheless not my will, but thine be done" (Joseph Smith Translation, Mark 14:36).[17] During Jesus' trial, the chief priests ask him, "'Are you then the Son of God?' He replied, 'You are right in saying I am'" (New International Version, Luke 22:70). Jesus' acknowledgment provides enough evidence for the Jewish leaders to seek the death sentence. From Matthew 27:50, Jesus' last words uttered in mortality testify of his relationship as the Only Begotten Son: "Father, it is finished, thy will is done" (JST). Thus both the birth and death accounts of Jesus testify that he is the Son of God.

"The Holy Ghost Shall Come upon Thee"

A key to identifying Jesus as the promised Messiah, at his birth and death, is his association with the Holy Ghost. John the Baptist makes this clear when he claims that the Messiah will follow him baptizing by fire (see Matthew 3:11). In the birth narrative, Luke mentions the Holy Ghost or Spirit six times; three from chapter 1 in conjunction with Zacharias (see Luke 1:15, 17, 41) and three connected to Simeon at the temple (see Luke 2:25–27). After the nativity narratives—except for the baptism, temptations, and one reference in Matthew—the Holy Ghost is not mentioned again in the New Testament until the Last Supper, when Jesus promises the Comforter.[18] Finally, after his Resurrection the disciples receive the gift of the Holy Ghost as Jesus "breathed on them, and saith unto them, Receive ye the Holy Ghost" (John 20:22). The Holy Ghost actively testified of the birth of the promised Messiah and then testified of his Resurrection.

"Emmanuel, or God with Us"

Throughout Matthew's Gospel, he uses structure to add meaning to his message. Matthew crafts his nativity narratives around five Old Testament citations as evidence that Jesus fulfilled Messianic prophecy.[19] His first quotation reference is Isaiah 7:14, "Behold, a virgin shall be with child, and shall bring forth a son, and they shall call his name Emmanuel, which being interpreted is, God with us" (Matthew 1:23). The verse is the only time that the Hebrew name Emmanuel is used in the entire New Testament. Matthew not only gives the name but also translates it. Matthew's account builds a correlation between the name at birth and the role at the Resurrection, when Jesus' disciples realized that God had been with them. The child Jesus is Emmanuel, "God with us," and after his Resurrection, Jesus states, "I am with you always" (Matthew 1:23; 28:20). The key element is Jesus is God—the babe in the manger, the boy in Galilee, and the man in Gethsemane. In the Passion narrative, we see Jesus as God overcoming the sins of the world and overcoming death. Jesus was a God speaking to a God as he pled, "O my Father, if this cup may not pass away from me, except I drink it, thy will be done" (Matthew 26:42). This was an appointment from a God to a God, and it was fulfilled as a God.

"Signs in the Heavens"

Both the birth and death accounts contain great signs that bear witness to important events. Luke's second chapter expounds on the shepherds' vision of angels: "The glory of the Lord shone" (Luke 2:9). Matthew reports that the unique star, which the wise men saw at its rising or "in the east," later reappeared as a guide from Jerusalem to Bethlehem (compare Matthew 2:2 with 2:9).[20] In addition to Matthew's new star and Luke's heavenly angels, the Western Hemisphere had "no darkness in all that night, but it was as light as though it was mid-day" on the night of the Savior's birth (3 Nephi 1:19). Samuel the Lamanite had foretold that "great lights" and many signs and wonders in the heavens would precede Jesus' birth (see Helaman 14:2–6). One of those great lights described in the Book of Mormon sounds similar to the wise men's star, "such an one as ye never have beheld" (Helaman 14:5).

In contrast to all this glorious light at Jesus' birth, no star shone in the Western Hemisphere at his death, "neither the sun, nor the moon . . . for the space of three days that there was no light seen" (3 Nephi 8:22, 23). In Jerusalem, Matthew explains that at Jesus' death, "darkness fell over the whole land, which lasted until three in the afternoon" (New English Bible, Matthew 27:45). The natural calamities personified the "gross darkness" of the people who "sat in darkness" (Isaiah 60:2; Matthew 4:16). In the Western Hemisphere, spiritual and physical darkness was made worse by "a great storm, such an one as never had been known in all the land" (3 Nephi 8:5). In Jerusalem, "the veil of the temple was rent in twain from the top to the bottom; and the earth did quake, and the rocks rent" (Matthew 27:51).

These tumultuous signs in the heavens at Jesus' death, together with the heavenly displays at his birth, mutually witness, in contrasting ways, to the eternal mission of him who created them.

"*Gold, and Frankincense, and Myrrh*"

The Magi offered the Christ child the gifts traditionally given to a king.[21] Early Christians thought the wise men's gifts foreshadowed Jesus' mission. Gold was interpreted as a gift for a king, thus setting the stage for Jesus to become King of Kings.[22] Frankincense depicted the divinity of Jesus.[23] In the ancient world, myrrh was used for embalming; therefore the gift was seen as preparation of Jesus' death, burial, and Resurrection.[24] After Jesus' death, John—the only Apostle at Jesus' cross—says that Nicodemus brought "a mixture of myrrh and aloes" for Jesus' burial (John 19:39).

In Matthew's nativity account, the Magi do not return to Jerusalem. King Herod realizes that "he was mocked of the wise men" (Matthew 2:16). The Greek verb *empaizō* ("mock") has a tone of ridicule. This strong language used by Matthew is employed again when Jesus is mocked and derided as a king during Matthew's Passion narrative: "When they had platted a crown of thorns, they put it upon his head, and a reed in his right hand: and they bowed the knee before him, and mocked him, saying, Hail, King of the Jews!" (Matthew 27:29; see also vv. 31, 41). This use of *empaizō* is another point of contact between the birth and death narratives. In addition to the word itself, the circumstances surrounding Jesus' birth are amplified in his death and draw a connection between the two witnesses.

Leaders "Seek the Young Child to Destroy Him"

The parallels between Jesus' birth and death continue in Matthew's text as they testify of his atoning sacrifice. When the angel returns to assure Joseph that the threat to Jesus' life is gone, the angel uses the plural: "*They* are dead which sought the young child's life" (Matthew 2:20; emphasis added). As we look back in the text to find the plural, we find Jewish leaders also mentioned. King Herod consults the "chief priests and scribes of the people" for information on the location of the new king that resulted in the killing the children around Bethlehem (see Matthew 2:4, 16). The phrase "chief priests and scribes" (Matthew 2:4) is not found again in Matthew's Gospel until Jesus' last week, when the "chief priests and scribes . . . were sore displeased" (Matthew 21:15) and plotted Jesus' death. In like manner, at the end of Jesus' life it is a group of leaders who try to kill Jesus, and "the chief priests and elders of the people" deliver Jesus to Pilate (see Matthew 27:1–2). From Jesus' birth, several were involved in plotting his death—whether directly like Herod or indirectly as accomplices.

In Matthew 2:13 we are told that Herod wished to "destroy" Jesus. In his Passion narrative, Matthew emphasizes the same word again: "But the chief priests and the elders persuaded the multitude that they should ask Barabbas, and *destroy* Jesus" (Matthew 27:20; emphasis added). Both threats against Jesus' life came at night (see Matthew 2:14; 26:47–56). The last link connects those babes slaughtered in Bethlehem for Jesus' sake with Jesus, who was killed for the sake all of God's children.[25]

ATONEMENT PROPHECIES IN THE BIRTH NARRATIVES

Up to this point, we have been drawing parallels between the nativity, Passion, and Resurrection accounts. These connections have been historical, natural, symbolic, and literary. An additional connection between the nativity story and the Atonement is through direct prophecy. As lucid as any other prophecies in the New Testament, Matthew's and Luke's birth accounts emphatically testify of the Lord as our Redeemer, Savior, sign of the Suffering Servant, solution to the Fall, and source of the Resurrection.

Redeemer. In Luke's narrative, the first words Zacharias speaks after his nine-month silence prophesy of salvation provided by the Redeemer: "Blessed be the Lord God of Israel; for he hath visited and *redeemed* his people, and hath raised up an horn of *salvation* for us in the house of his servant David" (Luke 1:68–69; emphasis added). The only other time Luke uses the word "redeemed" in his writings is just after Jesus' Resurrection on the road to Emmaus: "We trusted that it had been he which should have redeemed Israel" (Luke 24:21). The author carefully chose and placed his words to draw attention to the prophecy given at Jesus' birth and fulfilled in his atoning sacrifice and Resurrection. Zacharias also uses the word salvation (meaning the saving of our eternal souls) in the same prophecy. The word is not used again until after Jesus' Resurrection (see Acts 4:12; 13:26).

Savior. Early in Matthew's infancy chapters, Joseph's first angelic messenger prophesies that the Lord Jesus will "*save* his people from their sins" (Matthew 1:21; emphasis added). The

Greek *sōzō* can infer a general "rescue from danger or destruction" and more specifically a messianic deliverance or judgment.[26] All these meanings can be applied when the author repeats this word three times as Jesus is taunted in the cross: "Save thyself. If thou be the Son of God, come down from the cross. . . . He saved others; himself he cannot save" (Matthew 27:40, 42). The profane scoffers did not understand that not only would the Savior save himself in three days but also he would someday save them. A related word, *Savior,* is also found exclusively in Luke's nativity narratives. First, we find it in Mary's *Magnificat,* "My spirit hath rejoiced in God my Saviour" (Luke 1:47), and then in another angelic prophecy that the shepherds hear: "A Saviour, which is Christ the Lord" is born (Luke 2:11). The next time Luke uses the word Savior is after Jesus' Resurrection: "God exalted with his right hand . . . a Prince and a Saviour, for to give repentance to Israel, and forgiveness of sins (Acts 5:31).

Set for the Fall and Resurrection. Another prophecy that Luke records came at the temple forty days after Jesus' birth when Simeon holds the infant Christ in his arms and foretells, "This child is set for the fall and rising again of many in Israel" (Luke 2:34).[27] The Greek word *anastasis,* "rising," was translated by Tyndale as "resurrection" (see also Luke 20:27, 33). This alternative translation fits perfectly in the context with the verse: "This child is set for the fall and *resurrection* of many in Israel" (see Luke 2:34). This child was foreordained to save mankind from the fall (*ptosis,* meaning downfall, loss of salvation) and to provide a physical resurrection. Even though the birth accounts announce the arrival of the Messiah and King of Kings, it is not until Jesus' death and Resurrection that his disciples grasp that his kingdom was not of this world.

Sign of suffering. Simeon's Atonement prophecy at the temple continues, "Behold, this child is set for . . . a *sign* which shall be spoken against" (Luke 2:34; emphasis added). The literal translation of *sign* reads "a rejected (or opposed) symbol," referring to the rejection Jesus would experience during his mortality.[28] This reinforces Isaiah's prophecy seven hundred years previous regarding the Suffering Servant: "He is despised and rejected of men; a man of sorrows, and acquainted with grief" (Isaiah 53:3). Isaiah identified the sign—"I have graven thee upon the palms of my hands" (49:16). At the end of his life, the day before the Last Supper, Jesus identified himself as this rejected sign. The synoptic Gospels report Jesus' entreaty, "What is this then that is written, The stone which the builders rejected, the same is become the head of the corner?" (Luke 20:17; compare Mark 12:10; Matthew 21:42). The underlying significance of this prophecy was anticipated at his birth, but it was not fulfilled until his death. "With loud shouts they insistently demanded that he be crucified, and their shouts prevailed" (NIV, Luke 23:23, see also Matthew 27:21–23; Mark 15:12–14). Simeon's prophecy at birth was fulfilled as Christ became the Suffering Servant in his Passion and death.

CONCLUSION

Truly the nativity accounts are wonderful and beautiful. We love their simplicity, their forthright telling of the birth of Jesus. On closer inspection, the story of the Christ child's birth foretells what is to come during the events surrounding Easter. In addition to sharing the same season, the two accounts of Christ's birth and death share a similar message of suffering and redemption. From the first nativity passages, Matthew and Luke use their structure and stories to point to the great atoning sacrifice of Jesus as the Savior of the World. In this aspect, the Gospels share God's vantage point expressed in Moses 6:63: "All things are created and made to bear record of me, both things which are temporal, and things which are spiritual; things which are in the heavens above, and things which are on the earth, and things which are in the earth, and things which are under the earth, both above and beneath: all things bear record of me" (see also Moses 5:7; 2 Nephi 11:4; Mosiah 13:31; Hosea 12:10; Hebrews 8:5).

NOTES

1. Only Matthew and Luke share details of Jesus' birth in their accounts, and they were probably the last sections written in their Gospels. Fitzmyer and other Bible scholars deduce that the first things written were accounts of Jesus' death and Resurrection, then the Gospels were formed, leaving the birth accounts for last (Joseph A. Fitzmyer, *The Gospel According to Luke I–IX*, The Anchor Bible [New York: Doubleday, 1981], 305). Never do the rest of the four Gospels refer back to the unique information supplied by the infancy narratives. It is doubtful that the infancy traditions were widely known during the Savior's ministry, as is attested in various stories throughout the Gospels. It was assumed Jesus' literal father was Joseph: "Whence hath this man this wisdom? . . . Is not this the carpenter's son?" (Matthew 13:54–55). It was assumed he was born in Nazareth: "Some said, Shall Christ come out of Galilee? Hath not the scripture said, That Christ cometh of the seed of David, and out of the town of Bethlehem, where David was?" (John 7:41–42). Also, "Can any good thing come out of Nazareth?" (John 1:46; see also Mark 1:9). It was assumed he was human: "And they were all amazed, and spake among themselves, saying, What word is this! for with authority and power

he commandeth" (see Luke 4:33–37). With the helpful perspective of time, the infancy narratives were fashioned to testify boldly not only of Jesus' birth but also of his mission, death, and Resurrection.

2. Raymond E. Brown, *The Birth of the Messiah: A Commentary on the Infancy Narratives in the Gospels of Matthew and Luke* (Garden City, NY: Doubleday, 1993), 415. Brown also tells us that "savior" was a frequent title for subsequent emperors. Josephus recounts how the Palestinian city of Tiberius opened its gates to Vespasian and received him as "savior" (Josephus, *War*, 3.8.459).

3. Michael D. Coogan, *The Oxford History of the Biblical World* (New York: Oxford University Press, 1998), 522.

4. Josephus, *Antiquities*, 14.15.14, 16.4; 15.1.2, 8.4–5; 16.9.3–4, 10.1–2.

5. Literally Matthew 1:1 reads, "Book of the genesis" or "genealogy" of Jesus. Matthew chose to reflect the Pentateuch by opening his Gospel with the same title as the book of Genesis. This same word is also used at the beginning of his first scene in Matthew 1:18, but it is translated in English as "birth." By using the same Greek word *genesis* two times, Matthew strongly signals a connection with the Torah. Furthermore, this key word is used to form a relationship with the two sections and also the motif for the entire genealogy.

6. James E. Talmage, *Jesus the Christ* (Salt Lake City: Deseret Book, 1983), 81, 84–85; Bruce R. McConkie, *The Promised Messiah: The First Coming of Christ* (Salt Lake City: Deseret Book, 1978), 471; *Doctrinal New Testament Commentary* (Salt Lake City: Bookcraft, 1973), 1:94; Daniel H. Ludlow, *A Companion to Your Study of the Doctrine and Covenants*, 2:274; Ellis T. Rasmussen, *A Latter-day Saint Commentary on the Old Testament*, 260; Hoyt W. Brewster, *Doctrine and Covenants Encyclopedia*, 255; and others suggest that Luke's genealogy was actually Mary's lineage. They purport this to rectify the conflicting names and problem with Jesus being Davidic while only receiving Mary's bloodline. They assert that the genealogies in Matthew and Luke are actually Joseph's and Mary's lineages. This is contrary to what the scriptures say, though. Both genealogies in Matthew and Luke state they are of Joseph, not of Mary (see Matthew 1:16; Luke

3:23). Their proposal is also inconsistent with Judaic customs at the time, which honored only the father's genealogy as valid (usually women's genealogy was not kept, unless she was Aaronic). Having both from Joseph should not be a problem for Jesus being Davidic. During the Greco-Roman time period, when a Jewish man named a child, he legally adopted the infant. Modern readers may have a problem in identifying Jesus as "the son of David" without knowing if Mary was Davidic, but this was not a problem in the ancient world. Furthermore, Joseph's genealogy in Matthew included Ruth, who was adopted into the house of Israel and became David's grandmother. The assumption that Mary and Joseph were cousins is based on the possibility that Joseph's grandfather, mentioned in Luke 3:25 as "Mattathias" and as "Matthan" in Matthew 1:15, was actually the same person and grandfather for both Mary and Joseph. This theory is not based on the scriptural record, but it may be feasible. In the ancient Jewish world, marriages with cousins were common. Luke gives the only scriptural lineage of Mary when he states her kinship to Elisabeth, who was a direct descendant of Aaron (see Luke 1:5). Mary could be both Aaronic and Davidic, but the later is not recorded in the New Testament or the Joseph Smith Translation (JST).

7. Matthew carefully listed Joseph's ancestry to show the fulfillment of the Davidic prophecy. Matthew 1:17 demonstrates that the author tried to emphasize the number 14. He has organized the genealogy list to fit a formula. The spans of time covered by the three sections are too great to have contained only fourteen generations each. From Abraham to David there were approximately 750 years, from David to the Babylonian exile 400 years, and from the Babylonian exile to Jesus 600 years. One reason why Matthew used 14 is found in the Hebrew practice of finding numeric values for names. The numerical value of David's name, *dwd*, was 14, which is achieved when numeric values are assigned to the letters of the Hebrew alphabet in order: $d = 4$, $w = 6$, $d = 4$; hence $4 + 6 + 4 = 14$. From the fifth century BC, the accepted numeric value of David's name was 14 (Brown, *Birth*, 75). Therefore, with both names and numbers, Matthew shows that Jesus is a descendant of King David.

The number 14 is seen again as Matthew builds his gospel around fourteen Old Testament citations that testify Jesus was the promised Messiah.

8. Joseph Fielding McConkie, *Gospel Symbolism* (Salt Lake City: Bookcraft 1985), 199. Luke's record may be both plausible and unpretentious because he traces Joseph's lineage through Nathan rather than through the ruling kings.

9. Raymond Brown finds it significant that the most important names in Luke's genealogy often come as multiples of seven: David 42, Abraham 56, Enoch 70 and even God as 77 (*Birth*, 92–93). Richard D. Draper explains, "Biblical people squared a number to amplify its symbolic meaning" (*Opening the Seven Seals: The Visions of John the Revelator* [Salt Lake City: Deseret Book, 2003], 83). Thus seventy-seven would mean completely perfect.

10. The only other reference to an angelic visitation outside of the birth and Passion narratives occurs after Jesus' temptation. Matthew 4:11 describes, "angels came and ministered unto him."

11. Matthew's infancy account includes a total of five dreams; three specify an angel's presence (2:13, 19), and two mention warnings from God (2:12, 22). Four of the dreams are messages to Joseph and one to the Magi.

12. The angel Gabriel was identified by Joseph Smith as Noah (Andrew F. Ehat and Lyndon W. Cook, eds., *The Words of Joseph Smith: The Contemporary Accounts of the Nauvoo Discourses of the Prophet Joseph* [Provo, UT: Religious Studies Center, Brigham Young University, 1980], 8). Gabriel also visited the prophet Daniel (Dan 8:16; 9:21). Gabriel's annunciation to Mary and Elisabeth is very similar to angelic annunciations in the Old and New Testaments (see Matthew 1:20–21; Luke 1:11–20, 26–37; Genesis 16:7–12; 17:1–18:12; Judges 13:3–23). Brown isolates five steps they share: (1) appearance of an angel, (2) fear, (3) divine message is given, (4) objection by the visionary, (5) reassuring sign given (*Birth*, 259–69).

13. Luke uses *doulê* ("handmaid") twice in a voluntary, positive position (more like a servant). The second usage is in Acts 2:18: "And on my servants and on my handmaidens I will pour out . . . my Spirit; and they shall prophesy."

14. Isaiah 53:3 and 49:3, 15–16 are referred to as "Servant Songs."

15. This is the primary definition. It can also be translated, "a deacon, one who, by virtue of the office assigned to him by the church, cares for the poor and has charge of and distributes the money collected for their use; and a waiter, one who serves food and drink."

16. At the time of the angel Gabriel's annunciation, Mary was already "espoused" to Joseph. Jewish marriages took place at an extremely early age. Usually girls were betrothed between twelve and twelve and a half (Joachim Jeremias, *Jerusalem at the Time of Jesus* [Philadelphia: Fortress Press, 1989], 365). The ideal age for a young Jewish man to marry was eighteen (Jacob Neusner, *The Mishnah: New Translation* [New Haven and London: Yale University Press, 1988], Abot 5:21).

17. Scott H. Faulring, Kent P. Jackson, and Robert J. Matthews, eds., *Joseph Smith's New Translation of the Bible: Original Manuscripts* (Provo, UT: Religious Studies Center, Brigham Young University, 2004), 353.

18. Jesus asks, "If I cast out devils by the Spirit of God, then the kingdom of God is come unto you" (Matthew 12:28). Biblical readers often credit Peter's testimony to the Spirit, but the text credits the Father: "Flesh and blood hath not revealed it unto thee, but my Father which is in heaven" (Matthew 16:17). Any other references in the Gospels are to the future coming of the Holy Ghost. The word *pneuma* is also used for an "unclean spirit" and human spirit frequently.

19. Each of Matthew's five citations is preceded by the phrase "That it might be fulfilled." See Matthew 1:23 (Isaiah 7:14); 2:6 (Micah 5:2); 2:15 (Hosea 11:1); 2:18 (Jeremiah 31:15); 2:23 (Judges 16:17). In addition to citing five Old Testament scriptures that are fulfilled in his nativity, Matthew also has five dreams, five scenes, and mentions the word, "Christ" five times. Raymond Brown suggests that Matthew organized his nativity narrative to show a *new* law and then goes one step further to demonstrate how the old law is succeeded in the new law by quoting a "mini-Pentateuch" of five Old Testament prophecies that were fulfilled in Jesus' life (*Birth*, 48). The rest of Matthew's Gospel, chapters 3–25, includes five long sermons and is also organized around five "books," each ending with

the refrain, "when Jesus had ended these sayings" (Matthew 7:28; 11:1; 13:53; 19:1; 26:1). Brown continues, "These five books have been seen to constitute a Christian Pentateuch based on a typology between Christ and Moses (*Birth*, 48).

20.   The Greeks and Romans believed that the appearance and disappearance of heavenly bodies symbolized the births and deaths of great men. The idea was so broadly entrenched by the first century AD that Pliny felt the need to include a lengthy rebuttal in his *Natural History*. He combats the popular opinion that each person has a star that begins to give light when he is born and fades out when he dies (Pliny, *Natural History*, 2.5.26–6.28). This thesis was widely accepted for the births and deaths of great men. A late Jewish legend ascribed a star at Abraham's birth (W. F. Albright and C. S. Mann, *Matthew*, The Anchor Bible [New York: Doubleday, 1971], 14). The rising of a star or planet just before dawn was significant for Greco-Roman interpretation of certain incidents relating to prominent people (Ernest Martin, *The Birth of Christ Recalculated*, 2nd ed. [Pasadena, CA: Foundation for Biblical Research], 13).

21.   The number of Magi that visited the holy family has sparked interest throughout Christian history. Augustine and Chrysostom say that there were twelve (David Bercot, ed., *A Dictionary of Early Christian Belief: A Reference Guide to More than 700 Topics Discussed by the Early Church Fathers* [Peabody, MA: Hendrickson, 1998], 69). Others hold to a symbolic three because of the triple gifts. The apocryphal literature gives them names and countries and personal appearances. The Venerable Bede tells us "Melchior was an old man with white hair and long beard; Caspar, a ruddy and beardless youth; Balthasar, swarthy and in the prime of life" (F. W. Farrar, *The Life of Christ* [London: Cassell, Petter, Galpin, n.d.], 21–22). Some traditions maintain that Melchior was a descendant of Shem, Caspar of Ham, and Balthasar of Japheth. Thus they are representatives of the three periods of life and the three divisions of the globe. The gifts that the Magi offer are from Arabia. At the time, frankincense trees only grew in one place in the Arabian Peninsula. Gold and frankincense are gifts that Isaiah 60:6 and Psalm 72:10, 15 associate with the desert camel trains coming from Midian and Sheba (northwest and

southwest Arabia). The earliest traditions from the Christian fathers suggest the Magi came from Arabia. In AD 160 Justin wrote, "Magi came from Arabia and worshipped him" (Bercot, *Early Christian Belief*, 69). Forty years later, Tertullian deduced that the gifts were from Damascus and Arabia (Bercot, *Early Christian Belief*, 412). As early as AD 96, Clement of Rome associated frankincense and myrrh with "the East, i.e. the districts near Arabia" (Brown, *Birth*, 169). Palestine had close interactions with Arabia. From 120 BC to the sixth century AD, the kings of Yemen professed the Jewish faith (Alfred Edersheim, *The Life and Times of Jesus the Messiah*, 3rd ed. [McLean, VA: MacDonald], 203). In the Old Testament, the "people of the east" are desert relatives of Isaac and Jacob (Genesis 29:1). Men from the east had a reputation of being wise, and in 1 Kings 4:30–31 their wisdom is compared to Solomon's: "Solomon's wisdom excelled the wisdom of all the children of the east country."

22. By the time Matthew wrote his Gospel, the interpretation of *zahab* or gold as a metal was accepted (see Brown, *Birth*, 176). Gold is the precious metal most often named in the Bible (385 times). In the Old Testament, it was imported from Uphaz (see Jeremiah 10:9), Raamah (see Ezekiel 27:22), Sheba (see 1 Kings 10:2), Havilah (see Genesis 2:11), and Ophir (see 1 Chronicles 29:4; 2 Chronicles 8:18). Occasionally gold was acquired as booty (see Exodus 12:35; Judges 8:24) but more often through commercial enterprises (see 1 Kings 10:14–24). In the New Testament gold is used as a symbol of spiritual wealth (see Revelation 3:18). In John the Revelator's vision of heaven, the twenty-four elders were wearing golden crowns (see Revelation 4:4), and the New Jerusalem will be constructed of pure gold (see Revelation 21:18).

23. Frankincense is a fragrant gum resin exuded from the Boswellai tree. The tree grew on the Arabian Sea from at least 1500 BC (Lynn and Hope Hilton, *Discovering Lehi* [Springville, UT: Cedar Fort, 1996], 115). Frankincense was imported to Judah by camel caravan from Sheba (see Isaiah 60:6; Jeremiah 6:20). The Old Testament mentions frankincense as a perfume, occasionally used for secular purposes but most often for religious ceremonies. Exodus 30:34–38 contains the

recipe for a frankincense-based incense dedicated for ritual use. No other incense was permitted on the altar of the temple (see Exodus 30:9), and secular use of the sacred recipe was absolutely forbidden (see Exodus 30:38). Offerings of frankincense were set before the Holy of Holies with the bread of the presence (see Leviticus 24:7). It was also stored in the temple for later use (see Nehemiah 13:5,9; 1 Chronicles 9:29). Frankincense also accompanied cereal offerings (see Leviticus 2:1–2, 14–16; 6:14–18). In Revelation 18:13, frankincense is listed as part of the cargo of the merchants who weep for the fallen city.

24.   Myrrh is a yellowish brown to reddish brown aromatic gum or sap from trees that grow in Arabia, Abyssinia, East Africa, and India. It was highly prized from earliest times (see Genesis 37:25). It was used for incense and sacred anointing oil and as a perfume for garments (Exodus 30:23; Psalm 45:8). It was part of the cosmetic treatment used to purify young girls for the king's bed (Esther 2:12), and it was also used in Egyptian embalming (Mark 15:23; see David Noel Freedman, ed., *Anchor Bible Dictionary* [New York: Doubleday, 1992]).

25.   Brown, *Birth*, 204. The baby boys killed in Bethlehem are known as proto-martyrs because they were slain for Jesus' sake. King Herod also slew infant boys two years and under before in Syria as well—one of whom was his own son. Josephus lists Herod's atrocities, but nothing about a Bethlehem massacre is mentioned (Josephus, *Antiquities* 17.11.2). It may have been too small a crime to be listed among Herod's mayhem. Because of the high infant mortality rate, the maximum number of male children in Bethlehem under three years of age would scarcely have been more than twenty (Albright and Mann, *Matthew*, 19). The low number adds credence to its validity. The tendency in later writing was to exaggerate the number slaughtered. The early church father Justin has Herod ordering the slaughter of all the boys without mention of an age limit. The Byzantine liturgy sets the number of "holy Children" at 14,000. Syrian calendars of saints set it at 64,000 (Brown, *Birth*, 204–5).

26.   The authors of the Gospels use the word, "save," sōzō, several times (Matthew fourteen times, Mark thirteen, Luke seventeen, and John six), which does not detract from Matthew's tie at the beginning and ending of Jesus' life.

27.   The early Christian father Origen (c. AD 185–254) wrote his reflections of this verse: "For the falling of unbelievers and for the rising of believers. But only one who falls is he who had been standing. . . . For whose falling [did] the Savior come? . . . Perhaps the Savior came for the falling and rising of the same ones" (Origen, trans. Joseph Lienhard, *Homilies on Luke #17* [Washington DC: The Catholic University of America Press], 71).

28.   Fitzmyer, *Luke*, 429.

INDEX

Entries for images are indicated by italicized page numbers.

104–6; angels and, 107–8; obedience and, 108–9; divinity of Jesus Christ and, 109–10; Holy Ghost and, 110–11; Emmanuel and, 111; signs at, 112–13; gifts given at, 113, 123–24n21; leaders' involvement in, 114; contemporary knowledge of, 118–19n1; Matthew's narrative of, 122–23n19; Magi and, 123–24n21

natural disasters, 16–17

necklace, 83–84

Nephites, Jesus Christ visits, 9–10, 63

New Testament, treatment of women in, 62

Noah, 121n12

numerical values, 106, 120–21n7, 121n9

O

obedience: Atonement teaches importance of, 13–15, 19; of Jesus Christ, 108–9

Origen, 126n27

P

Packer, Boyd K., 91–92

Pantocrator, 46–47

parable: of lost coin, x–xi; of lost sheep, x, 51; of prodigal son, xi–xii; of wicked husbandmen, 16; of two debtors, 68–69

peace: Jesus Christ promises, 40–41; prepared place in

heaven as reason for, 41–45; knowing Heavenly Father as reason for, 46–48; Holy Ghost as reason for, 48–50; love of Jesus Christ as reason for, 50–53; during time of war, 54–58

Peter, 27–29

Pingree, Anne, 94

plan of salvation, Atonement as part of, 1–3

Pliny, 123n20

portraits, 85–86

prayer: Atonement teaches importance of, 5–7, 18; during Jesus Christ's visit to Martha, 29–30

prodigal son, parable of, xi–xii

R

Redeemer, 115

Rescue of the Lost Lamb, 82

Resurrection: event, 4–5; peace and, 56–57; Mary Magdalene and, 74–77, 79–80n11; James E. Talmage on testimony of, 96; prophecies on, 116

The Resurrection, 44–45, 95

reversals, ix–x

Richmond, Ron, 102

S

sacrifice: love as motivation for, 11–13; of Adam and Eve, 13–14